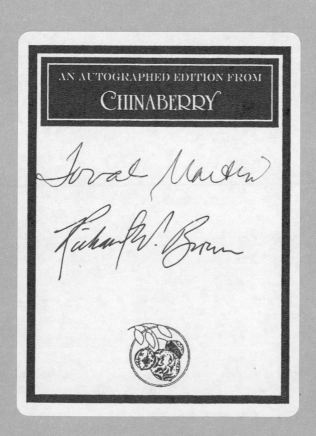

AN AUTOGRAPHED EDITION FROM
CHINABERRY

A TIME TO BLOSSOM

A Time to Blossom

Mothers, Daughters, and Flowers

Text by

TOVAH MARTIN

Photographs by

RICHARD W. BROWN

A Frances Tenenbaum Book

HOUGHTON MIFFLIN COMPANY

Boston New York 2001

Text copyright © 2001 by Tovah Martin

Photographs copyright © 2001 by Richard W. Brown

For information about permission to reproduce selections from this book, write to Permissions, Houghton Mifflin Company, 215 Park Avenue South, New York, New York 10003.

Visit our Web site: www.houghtonmifflinbooks.com.

Library of Congress Cataloging-in-Publication Data

Martin, Tovah.
    A time to blossom: mothers, daughters, and flowers / text by Tovah Martin ; photographs by Richard W. Brown.
        p. cm.
    "A Frances Tenenbaum book."
    ISBN 0-618-08615-3
    1. Flower gardening. 2. Flowers. 3. Martin, Tovah. I. Title.

    SB404.9 .M27 2001
    635.9—dc21   2001024475

Printed in Singapore
TWP 10 9 8 7 6 5 4 3 2 1

Book design by Susan McClellan

Books by Tovah Martin and Richard W. Brown

Tasha Tudor's Garden
Tasha Tudor's Heirloom Crafts
Garden Whimsy
A Time to Blossom: Mothers, Daughters, and Flowers

Books by Tovah Martin

Once Upon a Windowsill
Moments in the Garden
The Essence of Paradise
The Ways of Flowers
Well-clad Windowsills
Heirloom Flowers
Taylor's Weekend Guide to Window Boxes
Taylor's Weekend Guide to Indoor Gardens

Books by Richard W. Brown

Moments in Eden
Richard Brown's New England
Pictures from the Country
The View from the Kingdom
A Vermont Christmas
The Private World of Tasha Tudor
My Kind of Garden
The Soul of Vermont

CONTENTS

A TIME TO BLOSSOM

VEN WHEN I WAS VERY YOUNG, I WANTED TO WRITE a book. Before I could read words much longer than one syllable or pronounce my ballet teacher's last name, I wanted to write about a world dwarfed by hollyhocks.

I set up piles of paper, lined up sharpened pencils, and made myself an alcove on the Ping-Pong table, protected by stacks of A. A. Milne books from my sisters, who were playing Chutes and Ladders. And there I sat for what seemed like an eternity but was probably more like minutes, struggling to describe the exhilaration of climbing an apple tree and the pain of being impaled by a rose bush. I wanted to find words that would capture the thrill of being lost in a boxwood maze and knowing that the only hope of ever seeing my family again was a muffled giggle from somewhere deep in the distant shrubbery.

I wanted to describe the delphiniums, when their spires stood face-to-face with me; I wanted to write about why the poppies wouldn't wake up until after the morning cartoons. Somehow I knew that my

unique perspective on the garden would someday vanish, along with taking naps, sipping honeysuckles, chewing blades of grass, and many other good things in life.

I wanted to write about the tyranny of weeding and my strongly held conviction that lamb's quarters were admirable things that should be encouraged rather than eradicated. I would talk about planting marigold seeds with my mother and then waiting, waiting, waiting for an interminable twenty-four hours or more before sneaking out (against her strict orders) and scratching up the whole crop, only to expose tiny, shivering sprouts. Those are the lessons of a gardener.

There was wonder as I watched my mother's fingers deftly arranging flowers into bouquets; there was pride when I came home with armloads of daffodils harvested from my neighbor's back yard. And there was disbelief, even when I was young enough to have a seemingly infinite plausibility threshold, at the discovery that so much perfume could spew from the lackluster lips of a wallflower. I could believe in fairies; I could buy in to dragons, brownies, Santa Claus, and wishes on evening stars. But I was absolutely certain that someone had spilled something from my mother's vanity table all over the petals of that wallflower. I was no fool.

Meanwhile, a sense of immediacy compelled me to forgo several games of tag and lots of hide-and-seek. Somehow I must have known, even while I struggled to figure out how to spell "daffodil," that I would eventually lose the essence of how it felt to spend a rainy afternoon with my mother, pressing pansies or making scented geranium cake. And of course I was right. Although hollyhocks still hold some powerful magic, they aren't as surreal as they were when they towered tall overhead – though, amazingly, much of the splendor and mystique of the garden is still with me.

Mine wasn't a privileged youth, horticulturally speaking. My mother wasn't a world-class gardener, and she didn't tend a particularly large tract of land. But she always puttered around the back yard, planting this and that, and those moments flavored the rest of my life. We spent many hours outdoors together, planting seeds, transplanting seedlings, reading poetry on the porch, cutting flowers, folding linens; those were the things we did together, my mother and I. Those were the times when we blossomed.

Like many people's youth, my childhood was a whirl of tricycles and pin-the-tail-on-the-donkey, punctuated by huge bunches of lilacs plucked fervently on Mother's Day morning and then littered over half the countryside while I ran pell-mell inside. Somewhere in everyone's past is a moment when you stood by your mother's side and blew dandelions to see how far the parachutes would float, when your mother showed you the bee at the center of each delphinium flower. For some reason, these are the memories that linger. These are the times you never forget.

The smell of a cake baked with scented geranium leaves on the bottom never slips from your memory, especially when your mother let you sift the flour. You never lose the image of lilies glowing in the dusk, with the flush of lantern light on your sister's cheeks. Although much of youth slips away, these memories never fade. Over the years they gain patina, until you pass them along to someone else who is keen to know the mysteries of morning glories and hollyhock dolls. At long last, this is the book I started on the Ping-Pong table many years ago.

CHAPTER ONE

EARLY SPRING

 N A CHILD'S SEASONAL CALENDAR, EARLY SPRING leaves a lot to be desired. Filled with hope and promise, dreams and anticipation, it is a time when nature holds its breath, waiting for something to happen. For experienced gardeners, forced bulbs and potted primroses are promises that good things are about to unfold. But for those who have yet to establish a sense of order or who are not yet familiar with the schedule of events, early spring holds nothing but diversions. We drum our fingers; we bide our time and bond with allies. It is a time of closeness, of watching the world through the window. Even if we haven't yet witnessed many springs and we don't know that the crocuses will eventually push up through the snow, something in the air suggests that eventually, all hell is going to break loose.

FORCING BULBS

I HAVE MEMORIES OF WANDERING THROUGH GARDENS UNDER clouds of dogwoods. I can recall quite clearly the sensation of looking up at hollyhocks that dwarfed even my older sister. But those aren't my earliest memories of flowers. Before I was old enough to be left alone outside, when the whole world revolved around my mother, father, sisters, and home, I remember the refrigerator.

Everything that was delicious came from the refrigerator. It was the place I turned to when the world grew dismal and cranky. Few problems couldn't be solved by opening its door and fishing around on its shelves. Of all the formative sights and sounds, the refrigerator lingers most clearly in my memory.

For half the winter, it was monopolized by bulbs. We had to wedge the chocolate milk between clay pots holding buried grape hyacinths, tulips, or narcissus, trying not to jar them and send soil all over the Jell-O. It was a jubilant moment in early spring when my mother finally removed those pots from the path to the afternoon snacks. Before the first robins returned, the snow melted, or the crocuses poked through the patchy ice, before my mother packed us off to feed bread crumbs to the ducks, pots of paperwhites, tulips, and other forced bulbs brightened the house.

Like most of gardening, planting bulbs was a case of delayed gratification. Nothing looks quite as pitiful as a naked, gnarled, scaly daffodil bulb. If ever a chore seemed fruitless, it was potting these unpromising tubers in their heavy, shallow, thick-rimmed pots. In autumn, when we could employ our afternoons much more effectively by jumping into leaf piles, who wanted to fill squat terracotta pots with heavy, gritty soil, performing what seemed like an exercise in futility? In fall, I considered bulbs a colossal waste of time.

The magic began when they started to sprout. The paperwhites weren't much of a challenge. They weren't banished to the refrigerator and then rescued from the cold. Instead, these sissies of the bulb world were sent straight to the window and sprouted shortly after they were planted. They shot into immediate action, blooming their fool heads off and filling the kitchen with their eerie, mildly unpleasant smell, reminiscent of dirty laundry. Frankly, I wasn't really sure whether I liked or hated paperwhites.

FORCING BULBS

Paperwhites don't need to be chilled. Put them in soil or pebbles and set them on the windowsill, and they'll send up flowers a month or so later. Spring bulbs are another story entirely. Plant crocuses, tulips, daffodils, hyacinths, and grape hyacinths shortly after Thanksgiving, in gritty soil and snuggled close together in short, stout terracotta pots. Chill them for eight to twelve weeks in the garage, barn, or refrigerator – anywhere that remains a fairly steady 40 degrees Fahrenheit. After chilling, water them regularly, give them a prime position in the bright, indirect light of a cool window, and watch for signs of growth.

The daffodils and tulips were another matter entirely. At first they showed no promise at all. I could not figure out why my mother made such a fuss over a handful of pots that sat for months doing nothing. I always wondered what signal made her finally come to her senses and clear them from the refrigerator, leaving the space for desserts. Not long after she removed them, the annual magic began to unfold. It was, of course, far too subtle for my taste, but it had a faintly delicious quality nonetheless.

When the pots were stashed on the floor in some dark corner, small green blades began to break the soil surface. Suddenly one day little sprouts were just faintly perceptible, begging for a drink and a position in the sun. Even then they weren't given a spot close to the family's heart. Instead, they were banished to the cool sunporch, and my sisters and I were periodically sent out to serve them. Like little scullery maids, we went back and forth with watering cans in relays, trying not to slosh or dribble, satisfying the insatiable bulbs. That's when I would first discover the plump buds, and not long afterward the blossoms would appear.

The first flower was a big moment. At dinner, it was the centerpiece. When relatives came, it was trundled into some highly visible position. But pretty soon daffodils, muscari, and hyacinths were so plentiful that they were relegated to the kitchen table, where they overlooked the preparation of apple pies and witnessed after-school milk being spilled all over the cookies as we groped for a glass, lost in Nancy Drew. By the time they were in bloom – and the tulips always lagged behind everything else – they were no longer the great sensation.

When I think back, I realize that this procedure made the bulbs constant and comfortable companions, like the dachshund that was invariably underfoot. The pots came out of the refrigerator in succession, and by the time the tulips unfolded, the bulbs were firmly entrenched as members of the family. There was something wonderful about that, about walking by the daffodils and being so familiar with their company that you forgot to bury your nose in them. There was something so wonderful, in fact, that Daddy didn't complain, even when the hyacinths filled the house with their thick scent and made his eyes water and turn red.

DOLLHOUSE BOUQUETS

THERE WAS ALWAYS A BOUQUET ON THE TABLE. NO MATTER
what time of year it was, no matter how busy my mother happened to be, she always put flowers on the table. Granted, they were
slapdash affairs, with nothing studied about them. A bouquet might
be a bunch of columbines, a fistful of lilies-of-the-valley, or a cluster of
roses. Sometimes, when she felt daring, the medley was more exotic.
Often the bouquet was a pastiche of blossoms coming and going – the
few remaining dahlias from last week combined with some fresh glad-
iolas. No matter what anyone's opinion was on the combination of
orange marigolds and red zinnias, the flowers always brightened the
room. They were part of the interior scenery, just like the canary.

We learned to talk through them. Long ago my father had ceased
his habit of sliding the vase to the left or the right in order to see which
little girl was reporting on her triumphs during that afternoon's
spelling bee. We all became so accustomed to the challenge of speaking through a screen of carnations or zinnias that when the tabletop
arrangement was nothing more than a tray of blooming African violets, we felt slightly exposed. No guesswork was necessary when everyone was suddenly in clear view. Without the bouquet, dinner lacked
the element of mystery.

Often, especially on rainy days, I watched as my mother concocted
the bouquets. Newspaper was laid out on the kitchen table; there was
a hammer for crushing stems; and all manner of scissors, shears,
knives, and clippers were placed for easy access. As a prelude to the
action, a kind of opening prayer before my mother trimmed the first
stem or selected the right vase, we were requested in no uncertain
terms to be silent so she could concentrate. Then, with everything in
place, she proceeded to rip and tear at those flowers with a ferocity that
was a sheer delight to behold. Leaves flew, branches were beheaded, and
stems were shredded and bruised with a fervor rarely seen in my mother. It was exhilarating to witness the transformation of the kitchen
table into an unholy mess of extraneous petals and leaves, and there
was nothing like watching as harmony miraculously arose from chaos.

The results were not reproducible, of course. No matter how
deeply I concentrated on my mother's every move or how hard I studied the technique she used to jam the flowers into the wide-mouthed

crock, it was futile. In my hands, the stems toppled against each other, half of them falling to an untimely death on the floor, the rest forming a jungle of disparate shapes and colors. It was no use. My mother's vases were too ambitious for my motor skills; they gobbled up flowers. So I resorted to concocting something on a much smaller scale, and in that realm I excelled.

Back then, anything that was small was intriguing. The fact that the dollhouse held minuscule versions of the bureau in my bedroom, kitchen utensils in the pantry, and bric-a-brac in the parlor was the grist for my ambitions. Filling the tiny vase on the dollhouse's dining room table occupied many hours on rainy days (and rainy days are a nagging issue before you are in kindergarten).

Best of all, I was magically transformed into an incredibly adept florist when arranging those tiny bouquets. With only a fraction of my mother's furious energy, I could concoct equally impressive displays. And there was demand for the skill. The dollhouse needed fresh arrangements on a regular basis. It needed new blossoms in the windowboxes and flowers by the bedside. I rose to the occasion, and every bouquet looked a little better than the arrangement of the week before. Each one held a special splendor, a new nuance in color, and a lovely fragrance that captivated every doll who came to visit – even the dogs and the cats. And my mother was envious.

HOUSEPLANTS

REMEMBER WHEN YOU HAD TO STAND ON TIPTOES TO REACH the cookies in the middle of the kitchen table? Remember when you couldn't go to sleep without the company of three stuffed dogs, your favorite blanket, and a Raggedy Ann so threadbare that her face was held together with Band-Aids? That was the time when a philodendron played a formative role in my life.

As far as I can remember, the kitchen always entertained a row of African violets or geraniums, herbs or impatiens lined up on the windowsill. They were part of the decor, just like the toaster and blender. While the breakfast oatmeal was cooking, my mother would go back and forth from the plants to the tap, filling the pots with water or emptying their saucers as I watched from my stool, rubbing the sleep from my eyes and deciding whether I should top the oatmeal with a pear or a banana that morning.

The kitchen wasn't the only stronghold for plants – not by a long shot. In fact, it was an ongoing challenge to fit all the accouterments of youth – the rocking horse, the three-dimensional dinosaur puzzles, the model trains, my little sister's playpen – between the aspidistras, sansevierias, and dracaenas lurking in the corners. The dining room invariably held a few ivies trailing from the sideboard, quietly filling the space without drama or demands. A row of cacti, uncongenial and prickly, paraded across the window ledge in my father's study, off limits to my sisters and me, which made it difficult to appeal for sympathy when we emerged with our eyes filled with tears and our fingers

TAKING CUTTINGS

When a plant is clearly leaping to its doom, it's time to take cuttings. Both tips and segments of stems are salvageable, as long as they have the potential to make growth. Strip off any leaves that will be buried when you tuck the lower third of the cutting into the soil in a small clay pot. Keep the soil moist while roots begin to grow; covering the fledgling with an overturned Mason jar helps. Fast-rooting plants such as coleus can be plunked in a glass of water, but keep their head and shoulders safely above the water line. African violets, rex begonias, and sedums will form plantlets from nothing more than a leaf tucked in the soil. Bathroom and kitchen windows, usually more humid than the rest of the house, are ideal for the endeavor.

riddled with thorns. There were ferns in the living room, maybe a ficus or a ponytail palm standing on the sidelines of my early years. Wherever they were, whatever they were – whether busy Lizzies, angel-wing begonias, Easter lilies, poinsettias, or primroses that someone gave to my mother as a hospitality gift, or an orange tree that refused to set fruit – the houseplants provided companionship long before I was old enough to ride bikes with the neighborhood kids.

If the houseplants had been confined to the windowsills, then perhaps they wouldn't have made such an indelible impression. But they spilled into our play areas and were incorporated into games. When the shooter disappeared during a heated marble match, we recovered it by crawling under the fronds of the palm and the needles of the rosemary. They were part of the obstacle course that was the floor plan, competing with the overstuffed Naugahyde recliner and the china cabinet. When I curled up in the sun that came through the French doors, I shared the warmth with the spathiphyllums, Chinese evergreens, calla lilies, or whatever happened to be basking there at the moment; they were shifted around regularly.

The identities of all those plants – the primroses that came and went, the geraniums that stayed for a season, then left for their summer sojourn and never came back inside – may have slipped away, but a prevailing sense that those plants were an integral part of the family remains. They were carried to the sink regularly to be spritzed; they were pruned and groomed, their branches tied up and fussed over just as we were primped and polished. As they became taller, they were given larger shoes; as their hair grew, it was cut. They worked into the daily rhythm of sights, sounds, and activities. We were dispatched, especially when deep in the midst of a squabble or just on the verge of throwing a tantrum, to minister to their thirst.

Of course, my mother didn't keep the plants solely for our amusement and diversion. When adults visited, the conversation was filled with the lively exchange of remedies for the whiteflies on the poinsettias. But my friends never noticed the plants, unless it was to offer theories about what had provoked some philodendron or other to go crashing suddenly to its doom. And when I went to friends' houses, I didn't really notice their houseplants. Unless they had none. Then I wondered.

UNDER GLASS

WHENEVER I CATCH A WHIFF OF THE UNFORGETTABLE perfume of warm, moist soil mingled with the essence of fresh green leaves, I think of the greenhouses where I spent time dawdling as a child. Then another place where that scent predominated comes to mind: the inverted jars my mother used to start cuttings, nurture seedlings, and nurse limping plants along.

The glass nurseries were scattered throughout the house. In the kitchen window, a geranium cutting was often stashed under a jar, constantly monitored and coddled by my mother, off limits to me and my sisters. Protection from children's hands was not the main reason for housing plants under glass; it was merely a bonus. The primary idea was to give the feeble green patients a constantly humid and warm environment. Partially or completely closed to the outside air, plants required little or no care, needing only occasional water. As a result, the overturned jars were cracked open only so my mother could inspect their contents, primp or admire something, take something out or put something in. And that's when that wonderful smell – the perfume of warm earth, plunging roots, water droplets, and moist air – escaped.

If the overturned jars had held only invalids, they wouldn't have been quite so alluring. But they also nurtured valuables. A choice little something too delicate to trust in my proximity unless protected by glass, or too tropical to tolerate the sudden breezes when someone left the door ajar, was typical. Inside those glass jars dwelled fledglings and aliens, and therein lay their fascination. The temptation was to touch them. Failing that, at least I could try to gain a close look.

Closer inspection was not so easy. Half the allure of the glass nurseries lay in the fact that it was impossible to see clearly inside. You could, of course, drag a chair over to the window, climb on it, balance precariously, and crane your neck to get an inkling of what grew within. But the contents of the glass cases were invariably obscured behind a wall of water droplets. Condensation hung on the sides like a seductive screen, goading anyone with a moderately inquisitive nature to explore further. Fortunately, every once in a while a droplet would slither down like a teardrop, opening up a momentary chasm of clarity. Only then, if you were hasty, could you get a quick peek.

What you saw was the helpless, hopeless, and expensive. You saw tiny plants with half their branches broken off. You saw the cutting bestowed by your aunt, with numerous admonishments and instructions. And you beheld the slip of a dianthus dug up down the road, when your neighbor wasn't home, and housed behind glass for safekeeping until your mother devised some explanation for its migration past two stop signs and several sturdy picket fences into her garden. You encountered the rare orchid that cost a small fortune. And you watched plants recover, stretch their arms and legs, and eventually try to climb out of their nursery crib.

By necessity, everything was diminutive. The glass jars cosseted tiny plants in thumb- and thimble-sized pots, plants that never seemed to grow up, like the botanical version of Peter Pan. They harbored the begonia that was once overwatered and never forgave the indiscretion and the once-wilted and never reconciled primrose. But needless to say, when the plants grew large and sturdy enough to leave the nursery and join the world at large, they were no longer of any interest.

WARDIAN CASES

IN THE CENTER OF TOWN STOOD A ROW OF HOUSES FAR MORE self-important than our own. Big, forbidding structures, those homes could be entered only after you climbed a flight of cement steps, listening all the way up to the front door to a lecture on manners and not touching anything. Inside was no better. The rooms were not the sort of places that embraced those prone to dragging around their favorite tattered blanket; they were dark, stuffy, and dank, the walls lined with portraits of sour-faced relatives who looked down disapprovingly as a fragile old lady served tea and dried-out biscuits that couldn't hold a candle to my mother's chocolate chip cookies. And I said so.

Devoid of toys, lacking any visible diversion whatsoever, I had nothing to do in those houses but fidget and listen to the minutes being ticked away by the hall clock, praying for the moment when the hour would finally gong and my mother would gather me up, saying something about a piano lesson. And it was on one of those visits to just such a house, right when I was about to mention that I'd stopped taking piano lessons months ago, that I caught a glimpse of my first Wardian case, sitting in the corner by the large French door.

Of course, it wasn't until much later that my mother explained how Wardian Cases, a Victorian invention, were responsible for nurturing new introductions from the tropics, and how they became all the rage in prissy front parlors where, as far as I could see, they provided the sole diversion for anyone with some life left in her.

TWIGS

THE LOGIC BEHIND WADING OUT IN THE SNOW TO COLLECT armloads of bare sticks was not immediately apparent. It seemed that trudging into the fields in search of twigs in March was a good definition of a fool's errand. But you kept that opinion to yourself.

Of course, there were benefits to bundling up in leggings and boiled wool coat, stuffing your hair into a hat that would leave it snapping with static electricity, pulling on boots that would take long minutes to remove, slipping into mittens, and, thus fortified, venturing out into the frozen hinterland that was our back yard. There were advantages to trudging in my mother's bootprints past the far gate, beyond the fence, to territory that I hadn't explored in months. In the meantime, someone had been out there, sawing up the apple trees that came crashing down several snowstorms ago and stacking the wood. Clearly, every rabbit and its relatives had been enjoying a field day, judging from their tracks in the snow. In fact, evidence of all sorts of escapades – of breakneck squirrel chases, life-and-death cat and bird skirmishes, dog conferences – could be found in the melting snow. And now we were a part of history as well. My footprints following my mother's were now immortalized in the snow . . . at least until the thaw.

It wasn't the snowstorms that brought the twigs down, it was the ice. When it coated the branches and left them glittering and jewel-like, the ice looked lovely from a distance, but it wreaked havoc. Coupled with a brisk wind, it could prove lethal to any unsuspecting shrub. But it was ideal if you were interested in collecting branches.

Not all the branches volunteered; some had to be taken prisoner, and for that purpose my mother was armed with a handsaw and pruners, neither of which was ever left unattended near me. The pruners cut the branches, and the handsaw tidied up what remained so it would be ready to greet the growing season when spring finally arrived.

The exercise of forcing branches is tailormade for those who cannot wait out winter – and anyone under the age of twelve (as well as many much older than that) fits in that category. Shrubs, apparently, are also of an impatient nature and perfectly willing to be fooled into a flowering mode. A spring-blooming shrub needs only two months of freezing temperatures to swing into the serious business of blossoming, so branch collecting can begin as early as January, if anyone wants to risk the trek. Because a January expedition would easily have buried most of our reconnaissance party to their mufflers in snow, we usually postponed the deed until late winter, when my sisters and I had had our fill of snow-men, snow angels, and icicle-licking. When going out didn't entail the danger of an avalanche from the yew hedge or the risk of being speared by an ice dagger from the eaves, twig collecting commenced.

I couldn't help but wonder what my father thought as he watched the procession of naked branches coming inside. I thought my mother might have taken leave of her senses as I watched her labor for several hours, cutting and mashing stems and arranging sticks in her best vases with all the meticulous precision that she usually bestowed on flowers. When her work was done, the product looked very much like a bundle of kindling, elevated in status for no apparent reason.

Pussy willows and forsythias were the usual victims, cut for the purpose, but anything that had been felled by a storm was fair game. Apple branches appeared indoors regularly, as did redbuds and witch hazels. No matter what we brought in, two or three weeks went by before I stopped questioning my mother's sanity. Then, wonders happened.

To see a forsythia in spring is no big deal. To encounter pussy willows in April falls short of stopping the earth. But when you force those unpromising branches indoors, it's a different story entirely. Close up, each flowering branch has a grace that is totally lacking on the shrub or tree. Together, they form a bouquet that could easily have come right out of a fairy tale.

The fact that the flowers on our forced branches shattered without a whole lot of provocation was not to their credit. The trait that led them to create a path of petals through the house whenever we dragged them from one place to another was not their finest virtue. But my mother seemed to address the crisis with much better humor than she faced similar trails of dribbled oatmeal.

CHAPTER TWO

SPRING

 PRING FINALLY COMES, BUT NEVER SOON ENOUGH. Although all the world is drumming its fingers and chafing to sprout, the season itself is in no particular hurry – maybe because it knows we need time to clean out bird-houses and rake the stragglers of last autumn's leaves.

Spring sort of grows on you. The soul of discretion when it starts, it just dangles its toe in the water for what seems like an interminable length of time. And during those halcyon days, during the drizzly interludes that trap you indoors and the sun-kissed mornings when things poke their noses up above the soil, discoveries are made. Spring has to be approached with an open mind and a sense of wonder. And it is best explored together, because awe isn't necessarily inherent – it has to be learned, and that's where mothers come in.

Spring can't be trusted; you can't take its promises for granted. Everyone knows that. But no two springs are ever the same.

SUNDAY DRIVES

ON THE FIRST WARM SUNDAY AFTERNOON, WHEN SWEATERS were shed and shoes tossed off with little provocation, we were all packed into the old humpbacked Plymouth sedan to go bouncing down the road, headed nowhere in particular – the first trip of the season.

These were long, leisurely cruises along roads that twisted and turned, climbing and dipping, the kind of road that sometimes ended abruptly in someone's newly plowed cornfield or cut between a farmer's barn and his pasture so we had to wait while the cows moseyed across, staring at us through the car windows. Meanwhile, we were the proverbial Sunday drivers. My parents sat in the front, sedately discussing the scenery. My mother knit furiously all the time, dropping stitches when someone saw a robin, and we bounced around in the back seat.

Every once in a while, when someone's hair was about to get pulled clear out during a tussle or someone's favorite stuffed bear was in danger of being thrown from the window, my mother would calmly remark on the number of rabbits nibbling grass just to our right or ask my father to slow down so she could count the newborn lambs. But everyone knew that wasn't the real reason for the trip. Really we went in search of daffodils.

We weren't just seeking a newly installed daffodil or two shivering beside someone's mailbox – we were looking for expansive drifts of butter yellow that followed the contours of a forgotten field that no one ever mowed anymore. We wanted daffodils that had been planted by a foresighted farmer decades ago, to grow fruitful, multiply, and naturalize until they seemed integral to the scenery. Our mission was to ferret out those glistening oceans of daffodils that flooded the fields for a few brief weeks of splendor. Never mind the pitiful mess of foliage after the party was over; never mind the withered flower stalks and browned blossoms; never mind the decline. We went in search of the glory of spring.

The more the car was clouded by the dust of dirt roads and the more we bounced on poorly graded private lanes, the more likely we were to find a glorious superabundance caused by someone's long-ago investment gone wild. Masses of daffodils, hoards of daffodils, stampedes of blaring trumpets in their stiff colors that seemed slightly corny close up but looked ravishing when you passed by at a fast clip – that was the way to see daffodils.

There was no need to stop. No one begged for a bunch for the kitchen table, and no one had to wade between the leaf blades. Daffodils belonged to the countryside; they were best experienced when whizzing by, and that was that. Daffodils were the excuse to enjoy sparkling spring afternoons, to go nowhere and do nothing more than admire. No matter how tough times were, this was a joyous moment. It welled up in your throat and made you whoop and holler in glee. It incited all the back-seat fisticuffs and was responsible for all the mischief. Always, without exception, it made my mother put down her knitting and turn around in the front seat and say before even checking to make sure that we still had socks on, "Roll down the window, kids. Spring is here at last."

SPROUTS

FTER A FEW YEARS, THE TOP BUREAU DRAWER WOULD NO longer close properly because of the marigold seeds. Having long ago usurped the space for the sweaters, envelopes of marigolds increased annually to the point of overflowing. As much as my mother tried to stuff them back in and maintain a modicum of discipline in the drawer, the marigolds clearly had the upper hand.

It all began with a Brownie project. The packet from the revolving rack in the grocery store was selected solely on the basis of the alluring picture of sunny gold-and-brick-colored blossoms grinning on the front. If I had chosen delphiniums, the family wouldn't be maneuvering gingerly around uncompromisingly orange flowers stuck in every patch of garden that I could appropriate. If I had gone straight for delphiniums, that would have been the end of it. Even if they didn't die outright, they would never produce the progeny that the marigolds fostered. Years later, when my mother stood in the center of my bedroom with furrowed brow and a sizable stack of displaced sweaters, she definitely regretted the day she let marigolds into our lives.

Whether it was impatience or practicality that prompted me to sow the seeds indoors, I can't recall. But I do remember innumerable seed flats, each stuffed with as many marigold seeds as I could possibly scatter on the surface (at a certain age, "sow thinly" is not in your vocabulary). I'm sure that my mother oversaw the project. But then, she was a strong proponent of ridding the house of as many extraneous marigold seeds as possible. She might have been prone to munificence.

Never mind all the vigilance necessary to keep the seed flats moist but not soggy during the days right after they were sown. Never mind the shuffling back and forth to provide heat and sun, but not too much, before they even revealed signs of life. The work really began when the seedlings had to be transplanted.

Throughout most of the year, my mother transferred plants from smaller to larger pots with a few deft movements and much flying of potting soil, a process that was mildly intriguing but certainly couldn't hold my attention. Seedlings were a different story. Anything defenseless, spindly, and in need of nurturing holds a certain fascination, and the marigold seedlings definitely fell into that category.

Maneuvering their thready roots into the tiny pots that were their starter homes and manipulating the foliage so it wasn't bruised or bashed beyond recovery posed a significant challenge. Getting the right end up was also a feat, as was repairing all the bruises and scrapes along the way. Of course, watering each seedling rigorously after transplanting helped prevent the air pockets that are bound to result when someone with limited dexterity dabbles in tasks requiring fine motor skills. And that was just the beginning. Transplanting was followed by the substantial burden of remembering to care for the seedlings after they were given their limping start. The whole exercise was not unlike motherhood.

There was one consolation, though: there were plenty more marigold seeds where those came from. And I held tenaciously to that solace. After the marigolds had been safely transplanted, developed their first set of deeply cut leaves, and begun showing signs of flowering, it was suggested that perhaps the marigold-seed stockpile could be dispensed with. The subject was broached during cookies and milk, when it was assumed that my guard was down. Only the slightest sign of consent would enable my mother to disperse the seeds to worthy recipients throughout the developing nations (which was where she swore they would go). But the marigold seeds were not negotiable. If a shortage of dwarf French marigolds ever occurred in the world, I would be ready and well stocked to stave off the emergency. Indeed, if my crop failed owing to my own clumsiness or acts of God, I was ready.

When the little marigolds were established and the world was warm, sunny, and prepared to receive them, they went outside. I planted them wherever a spot could be found. You can be sure that if there was the slightest gap in the foundation evergreens, a glaring golden marigold popped up in the vacancy. If the smallest pause occurred between the geraniums in the windowbox, a marigold stepped into the position. My mission, as I saw it, was to perpetuate marigolds. I liked to think of myself as a small, female, curly-headed version of Johnny Appleseed.

I haven't the faintest idea what happened to all my marigold seeds. As far as I know, they're still in the top drawer of the bureau. I like to think that they remain, waiting to be pressed into service. Maybe my mother slowly used them up, planting them year after year. I know that I haven't consented to their removal. But then, my mother hasn't asked in a while.

PANSIES

I REMEMBER PANSIES. DOZENS OF SAUCY FACES, EACH ONE more compelling than its neighbor, called to me at Mrs. Logee's greenhouse or at the market down the street, begging for adoption.

While my mother was preoccupied with picking out onions in another aisle of the corner market, I was left to ponder the pansies. That took both time and concentration, because I hoped that if I sneaked a pot into her shopping basket, the pansies' sheer pluck would capture her heart. But one pot always led to another, and pretty soon at least half a dozen pert faces – some bewhiskered, others streaked, solid, blotched, banded, bewildered, impetuous, and impertinent – were waiting for my mother when she returned with the onions. At least half a dozen, and I exercised such restraint. But I simply could not settle for less. As I told her, in no uncertain terms.

Pansies are like snowflakes or the faces of your friends – each one different, all with something in common. That's the beauty of them: they play as a team. There's no sense in having pansies unless you collect a crowd of many little hooligans to battle it out in the garden. Pansies are the ones who conquer spring by stampede.

So the time inevitably came when we had amassed a surfeit of pansies. We crammed them into little pots and bigger pots, old kettles, windowboxes, olive oil tins with their tops shorn off, anything that might hold soil (and many things that probably wouldn't hold soil very long). Their fleetingness was half the charm. Pansies only blossom strongly in the cool of spring and autumn, flagging, as we all do, when the temperatures soar. They never burden your attention for too long. So we treasured them briefly on the windowsill in the chilly breezeway (my sister never remembered to close the door), and when the weather moderated, we tucked them into every crevice of the garden to fend for themselves. While spring still sent goosebumps in the evening, pansies peeked from dimly lit spots and sparked a glimmer even in the stern eye of the neighbor who marched over to complain when our rabbit devoured his flowers.

That's when my mother proved her worth. On rainy days – not on drizzly days, but when spring showers were truly torrential – she found employment for all those pansy flowers, freezing them in ice cubes or pressing them between the pages of the dictionary or any equally boring volume that no one ever consulted. Who could remember all the books where pansy flowers had been stashed on a rainy afternoon? For the rest of our lives – certainly for the remainder of our educational careers – they came spilling from the *Britannica* or the atlas whenever we looked up the population of Mongolia or the whereabouts of the Rub' al-Khali.

Knowing that later we would find bits of pansies strewn throughout life, my mother got her mileage from these springtime musketeers. She handed out crayons so we could draw long, elegant dresses and gallant trousers, to which she affixed pansy faces. When we got tired of that, she took out the pansy rings. We filled these terracotta rings with water and floated as many cut pansy flowers as we could fit in them, then set the rings on the supper table, for the moment when my father would come home.

PRESSING PANSIES

Pick pansies for drying after the sun has burned the dew off the flowers but before they have begun to wilt. Then snip off their stems, lay the flowers absolutely flat between sheets of wax or tissue paper, with plenty of space between blossoms, and place the whole thing between the pages of the largest, heaviest book in the house. Leave the pressed flowers undisturbed and flat for at least two weeks, preferably longer. Years later, long after you put the project out of sight and mind, the flowers will flutter from the pages like confetti.

TULIPS

I ALWAYS FOUND TULIPS REFRESHINGLY AWKWARD. STRETCHING their long and lanky stems, balancing their blossoms on top of gangly, slender stilts, they took a stab at grace but invariably failed. It was an admirable quality, and I could sympathize. They rushed up in a spurt of enthusiasm and for a few sparkling days they raged, running around in ridiculous colors and stopping cars with their acrobatics. Of all the flowers in the garden, tulips were the ones that turned cartwheels and did handstands. For a while they were cheerleaders, but then they were sidelined by a cloudburst.

When the sky started to show a dark mood and the clouds began to congregate thickly and swirl in murky cohorts, we were allowed to cut the tulips. After my mother rushed around slamming windows, pulling the clothes off the line, calling the cats in, and stuffing the dog safely in the bathroom, then, if the rain hadn't started, we followed her out to salvage the tulips. It was a thrilling moment, decapitating flowers in the flush of their prime and tossing them into aprons while the wind gathered and billowed the outstretched aprons and their contents. This glorious juncture of bedlam and blossoms always ended in a race with pelting raindrops, leaving scattered petals in our wake.

In the pantry we ran towels through our hair and changed into dry clothes, and then we stood on stepstools by the kitchen table to witness the effort to save the tulips. Pitchers, Mason jars, the vase with the nick from the excitement during last year's thunderstorm, were all lined up to receive the refugees. That's where the tulips came into their splendor and were transformed into swans.

Not immediately, but the next morning, the metamorphosis was evident. Suddenly the former clowns were all ballerinas. Their stems curved in the first and only graceful pirouette of their brief lives. My mother might try to straighten them in the vase, but it was hopeless. They would never again stand stiffly at attention.

No longer awkward, the rescued tulips lived the rest of their allotted time in sheer elegance. And when their petals dropped, they didn't spill in a sudden shower of embarrassment. They fell eloquently, one at a time, floating down and curling like apple peels reflected in the polished wood of the mahogany dining room table.

CUTTING TULIPS

The way to extend a tulip's vase life is to cut the flowers before they open fully. To convince them to stand straight, you can wrap them in a newspaper up to the chin, but such efforts are usually wasted. Tulips just tend to slouch. Anyway, they don't last forever. You can postpone the inevitable by bunching them tightly in the refrigerator, but the stems and leaves turn a sickly shade of pale without light. It's better to become resigned to both their posture and their brief lives.

MAY BASKETS

Mrs. Logee, the florist down the street, made May baskets. With a few swift movements of the wrist, she seemed to throw the baskets together. Of course, the occasion didn't permit the luxury of a lot of fussing – the whole thing, from picking the flowers as early as you could rise to delivering the baskets, was confined to the daylight hours of May 1. So with a sense of urgency Mrs. Logee snipped stems, stripped extraneous leaves, and slit and smashed lilac stems so the blossoms wouldn't wilt. We watched, transfixed, as she readied dozens of baskets for their precarious journey past an obstacle course of tricycles, skates, and Doberman pinschers to be tied to knockers throughout the neighborhood.

As she worked, Mrs. Logee provided her little audience with a running litany of May-basketing advice and exhortations. Like football plays or battle strategies, her maneuvers were never left to chance. Not only did she describe precisely how to achieve the sneak attack on the front doors, but she spilled all her secrets, including why she selected 'Angelique' tulips ("Because double tulips don't shatter") and how tightly furled a ranunculus must be to unfold gradually after the basket was discovered. We received and filed away all this in whatever part of the brain stores data that won't be accessed for years. More entertaining and timely by far was watching Mrs. Logee's nimble fingers turn daffodils upside down and fill their hollow stems with water or snip off the tips of young stocks so they wouldn't keel over in the time it took to secure a basket to a doorknob.

Whether we were invited to participate or not, we all tried our hands at May baskets, with varying degrees of success. The baskets were filled with pint-sized plastic reservoirs to hold water (Mrs. Logee had been saving margarine containers for months for the purpose). Dull-nosed scissors in hand, we beheaded blossoms, tore off petals, and ripped spires into smithereens. Meanwhile, the work table (and the floor below) resembled precisely the scene that would have resulted if a tornado had come and gone. The mess was also part of the May Day tradition.

Our presence was tolerated, if not actually encouraged, because delivery couldn't be accomplished without us. When the last tulip had been tucked between lilacs and anemones and the final product looked much too good to give away, we were sent home to change clothes. Then Mrs. Logee's messenger service was dispatched to cover the neighborhood.

The whole idea was to be swift. Stealth was needed to sneak up to the knocker, tie the basket to the knob, and vanish into thin air. A technique was required. A plan of slipping from shrub to hedge to stoop to knocker was mapped out and implemented with split-second precision. The maneuver could not have been accomplished more brilliantly by an ambush squadron. But still, I had to wonder. Why were we wearing our prettiest party dresses and toe-pinching Sunday shoes to ring the doorbell and run?

We never received thank-you notes afterward. May baskets were wrapped in anonymity, which explains why no one admitted that they'd spotted a familiar head of curls disappearing around the corner of the foundation planting. But everyone gave Mrs. Logee a wink at the post office the next day.

APPLE BLOSSOMS

MY MOTHER WAS NOT A MAJOR ADVOCATE OF CLIMBING trees. In fact, I can't recall a single time when she went out of her way to encourage that activity. In her estimation, children belonged firmly on the ground. Period.

So I discovered trees on my own.

It all started with an apple tree. I remember that tree vividly, silhouetted in the field halfway to school, stooped by time, its long, low-slung limbs swooping down in expansive gestures. For a long time, it held no interest for me except for the fact that it furnished shade for a Shetland pony. But that changed.

At nine years old, you can't help but harbor mixed emotions about trees, especially an apple tree composed (as apple trees often are) of arthritic joints and gnarled, distorted boughs stretching out to snatch you up, never to be seen by your friends and family again. To a child, an apple tree could be classified in the same category as the stranger she was told to avoid. When several of them ganged together in an orchard, they seemed like a band of bad actors. You had to mistrust trees at first. And it just grew worse when summer passed, leaving all the apple tree's bony limbs exposed and beckoning.

But then there was spring. And apple blossoms.

Lost forever is whatever instant of pluck or curiosity provoked me to climb the apple tree for the first time. Maybe I did it out of sheer defiance, or because I was tired and the ground was wet, or simply to smell the apple blossoms or inspect them up close. I left my schoolbooks and the pony below and maneuvered onto a lower branch. From that perch I saw another branch conveniently placed a little higher, and another, and another, until the pony was obscured by pinkish white blossoms far below.

After that, all trepidation evaporated into thin air. The bony limbs that once seemed fiendish became friendly; clumsiness became grace. You learn the apple tree's body language, and it recognizes your hand-hold and footprint. When you stand in its shade, that's friendship. But when you're up in its boughs, you and the tree are one.

Every tree has its unique climbing path, a specific combination of footholds and handholds leading to scraped knuckles and bruised

knees. The apple tree and I choreographed a singular combination of jumps, swings, grasps, and footwork that made us partners in crime. After that, it never varied. It was like our password.

I could weave a long story about how it felt up in the tree – about the way the breezes differed from those on the ground, about forgetting to worry about losing my balance and giving myself over to daydreams. About trust. About the time I spent pretending that I was comfortable straddling a limb, my back pushed against rough bark, until I truly *was* comfortable, surveying the world from a canopy of leaves. About hiding up there, strategically positioned where no one would think to look, able to drop apples on unsuspecting passersby with complete anonymity. If you think back, you'll remember the same arboreal understandings and recall just how it felt in your apple tree.

Once you've climbed your first apple tree, you climb a lot. For years you size up every tree you encounter for its climbability. Then suddenly it ends. Just as one day your little sister unaccountably ceases to run headlong everywhere and begins to walk demurely instead, one day you stop compulsively climbing trees. For no reason, you lose the urge that drove you up. You forget the sensation of being a limb among limbs, a bough among boughs. It disappears entirely.

Then comes the day when you find yourself discouraging your daughter from climbing trees. You explain earnestly that she's better off on terra firma. You talk about broken bones, stitches in the emergency room, and how long it takes a skinned palm to recover. You say all those things to her knowing full well that she'll meet her apple tree someday and disobey.

MOTHER'S DAY LILACS

For certain there would be lilacs for cutting by Mother's Day. They would be bearing their fat clusters of powder-colored blossoms, just ripe for clipping, so convenient for a bouquet.

The weekend before Mother's Day, I always went shopping for a trinket for my mother. With my father or an aunt, I picked out a necklace or a bracelet that they imagined she might enjoy. But deep inside, I knew that my mother would really prefer a giant armload of lilacs. They would bring the biggest smile; they would make her eyes well up in sheer pleasure. That was why I sneaked out on Mother's Day morning, barefoot and still in my nightgown, before anyone was awake or my hair was brushed, to fetch lilacs.

Every house I have lived in has had lilacs lolling around somewhere, usually leaning against the back porch or lurking near the front door where the wind might carry the fragrance inside. They were gangly, leggy, and easily overlooked most of the year. When they weren't laden with their lavender blossoms, who noticed them? Except when they drooped in a drought or became dusted by mildew in the mugginess of high summer, they neither drew the eye nor begged for attention. The bushes lacked grace, which made you love them all the more. And their faults were easily forgiven in the flush of flowering. But most critical for my purposes was the timing. They were reliable. They'd be there on that Sunday morning – you could set your watch by it.

Even on tiptoes, I could reach only the lower branches on shrubs that stretched taller than the front porch roof. But with a little effort, I could bend some flexible branches down to retrieve the plumpest clusters. That is, until my free hand became too busy holding on to its impromptu bouquet.

And that's really why I loved lilacs: because they fell naturally into a bouquet. They demanded neither skill nor dexterity to harmonize into an arrangement of luscious colors more beautiful than any florist could possibly compose. No ribbons, no tying of bows, no fumbling with filler was required. Lilacs were exquisite all alone. When that clutch of flowers was flourished with great fanfare from behind your back, your mother would smile – she would always smile, and love it.

Later I learned how to strip and smash the stems. Later I discovered how to make a lilac bouquet that would last longer than a few days of wonderful-smelling splendor. But initially, the only lilac bouquets within my capacity were incredibly evanescent. For just a couple of twilights, the aroma traveled with the fluttering of curtains from the dining room table to my bedroom. After a few days and a few lamplit evenings, the blossoms would be wilted beyond consolation. But then, nothing in spring was meant to last, least of all the lilacs.

Making Lilac Bouquets

Without special care, lilacs will swoon before you can get them safely into a vase, and that's why you should cut them in early morning or at dusk, when only three quarters of each plume is open. Take a bucket of water outdoors, scrape the bark from the lower two inches of stem, and dunk the stems immediately into the bucket. Even lilacs that are wilting can be revived by plunging the stems in hot water for one minute, but wrap a dish towel around the flowers to protect them from the steam. Then recut each stem at an angle, slice it up the middle, strip the bark that will be submerged in water, and smash the stem with a hammer. It's not a pretty business.

DANDELIONS

WHY THE WORLD WAGED A VENDETTA AGAINST DANDELIONS was beyond me. Few sights were as satisfying as a lawn spangled with a confetti of gold. As I pointed out to my father at every possible opportunity, dandelions looked stunning from a distance, and they were gorgeous close-up as well. I could not understand why he rushed out with the lawnmower to chop off their heads before they formed seeds. To me, the seedheads were the best part.

Clearly, action was necessary. So I made it my goal to get out there and blow every flossy orb skyward well before the weekend. Few things compared with the gossamer parachutes floating lackadaisically on a light midsummer breeze. A single breath from my lips, a quick twirl around with a dandelion magic wand, and a feathery blizzard followed. It was better than a pillow fight, and lacked the repercussions or the burden of cleanup when the party was over. The notion of nipping this amusement in the bud was just plain irrational. Dandelions provided the first in a series of signposts that made me wonder about the effects of age on the faculties of reason.

Dandelions made an equally fine accent in the garden beds. Why my mother brought home wagons filled with potted plants of inferior splendor and banished all the brilliant gold dandelions was another of the mysteries of childhood. Besides, her favorite flowers, the ones that she had conniption fits over when someone mistakenly yanked them out, were the ones with the shallow root systems that surrendered easily to the slightest tug. Weeds, in contrast, had a tenacious grip on the soil and wouldn't let go without considerable tussle. Dandelions, carpet weeds, and witchgrasses were survivors. Unlike all the foolish flowers that required protection from every chilly night with draped sheets and outspread newspapers, weeds were smart enough to sprout after the last snow. Weeds would inherit the earth.

Weeding was an exercise in futility. Only a few days after we had scoured a segment of the garden for weeds, there they were again, proof that spontaneous generation was alive and well in our back yard. This was nothing short of a miracle, and it seemed both wise and prudent to let nature take its course. If raspberries were hell-bent on monopolizing the iris bed, then who were we to stand in their way? And if the irises seemed perfectly willing to surrender their turf, it was meant to be.

But my mother wouldn't have it. She absolutely refused to see reason. Consequently, I came to realize that my parents held fantasies too. They took part in the same games as I did, but on a different scale. Although my mother had long since ceased to play with dolls, she nursed her garden, vanquishing the bullies and fighting off marauding gangs. The reason that the garden held her fascination, I began to see, was that it was filled with weaklings. Delphiniums required coddling, but the weeds could get along fine without her. She was just being a mother.

SWEET PEAS

ONE YEAR THE SWEET PEAS LASTED INTO SEPTEMBER, BUT that wasn't usually the case. More often, by the end of July they were a tangled mess of withered stems barely supporting flagging blossoms. But their transience in no way diminished their fascination in my eyes. If anything, it intensified the attraction. There was something very savvy about any flower that chose to avoid the languid, sweltering days of summer. It was a very smart move in my book.

Sweet peas were full of intelligent decisions, as far as I could tell. For example, a sweet pea corsage usually wilted long before graduation was over. By the time the second or third speech was under way, in fact, it was in a dead swoon. And by the time the graduates were filing out, diplomas in hand, all of the sweet pea corsages in the class were sagging precipitously. It was a glorious sight.

But that didn't stop mothers from bending over to pin sweet peas on their daughters' chests before they were lined up by height to file onto the bleachers. The fact that these corsages would never last out the ceremony in no way affected their popularity, because when the students proudly paraded in, before fidgeting through the speeches and steadying their ridiculous headgear against the gale-force gusts that always seemed to rise, the sweet peas were absolutely breathtaking.

Of all the scents of childhood, of all the memories of freshly baked muffins on Sunday mornings and gingerbread cookies whisked out of the oven, nothing lingers with the same intensity as the perfume of heirloom sweet peas. This signature scent – honey, hot wax, and vanilla – is the elixir that haunts every late June. The scent is strongest, conclusive tests have shown, just before your corsage wilts.

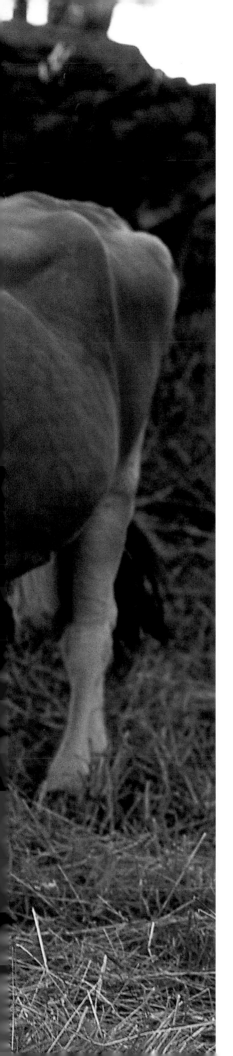

CHAPTER THREE

SUMMER

THERE ARE NO MOMENTS OF BOREDOM IN EARLY summer. Exhaustion, yes. Restlessness, maybe. But not boredom, because there is something boundless about the first days of summer. Anything can happen. The season can go anywhere. Plants shoot up like beanstalks and blossom with an indecent profusion. First they parade around in regal splendor, and then they stampede. Summer is bursting at the seams. If you follow suit and run around harum-scarum, who can blame you? You are merely following summer's lead, and so is everyone else. Summer is mass hysteria.

Everyone seems the same age in early summer: young. And everything overflows with exuberance and expectation. When things are very young, they toddle, taking little, uncertain steps. Then they run, and everyone has to chase them. That is the essence of early summer. It is a time when we all scamper and stretch and overflow our boundaries and blossom together. There are no limits in early summer.

POPPIES

THE FACT THAT POPPIES RARELY TURNED UP WHERE THEY were invited was a big fact in their favor. The trait that led them to pop up wherever their resolute little minds decided to not only demonstrated the pioneer spirit but showed a strong tendency to discount authority. Secretly, you cheered such freewheeling acts of civil disobedience. And deep in her heart, so did your mother.

Poppies sprouted wherever they felt like colonizing. Never singly, always in mutinous hordes, they infiltrated the cornfield as well as the perennial border and emerged on the breakneck hill that couldn't be mowed as well as in crevices between the bricks of the patio. Considering my mother's surprise at their inventiveness and the fact that I was continually being interrogated about taking liberties with the seedheads (which, given the opportunity, I distributed in the same spirit in which I dealt with the dandelions), I felt fairly certain that the omnipresent poppies hadn't been sown purposely by any human hand. During those early years, my tendency was to jump straight for supernatural forces.

Besides their penchant for thumbing their noses at propriety, other traits unique to poppies fostered camaraderie. First of all, they slept late. The Shirley poppies never unfolded until after you'd finished watching the morning cartoons. Of course, when they did open, their blossoms were far too fragile for my taste. For close companionship, I was more apt to choose the kind of flower that would remain intact when you clutched it by the throat and ran around the block a few times waving it in the breeze. But you can't have everything.

All sorts of poppies punctuated the different spurts of summer. Shirley poppies were red and hemmed with a thin white edging, while corn poppies came in different shades of coral. Lettuce poppies held a crinoline of many petals at their core, and Oriental poppies were large, gorgeous, and early, but few sights were as pitiful as the charred remains of an Oriental poppy after its brief appearance. California poppies were another matter entirely. All the poppies shared one defining characteristic: they were dead set on taking over the universe.

Poppy seeds were traditionally sown just before the last snow to give them the cool, damp conditions they prefer, but these invaders were the epitome of patience, sometimes lying in the soil for years

waiting for the ideal conditions to germinate. They loved newly disturbed soil, the kind of earth that you got after you did the spring removal of winter's debris with a rake. When they sprouted, they looked like the botanical version of hair on a dog's back at first, and the seedlings were equally dense, eventually developing their true blue-green leaves from weedy-looking beginnings. At that point they had to be thinned to at least two inches apart and given plenty of sun in a well-drained soil.

Given those conditions, they tended to spread their progeny over your yard, your neighbors' yards, and your friend's yard in the next town. There wasn't a poppy on earth with scruples.

Still, they were easy enough to weed out. When too many poppies invaded, my mother sent us outside and paid good money to pick out every one – or to thin them without disturbing the larkspur that had also seeded itself in. There was a lesson to be learned in that. Gardening was really about selection. In fact, life was about selection, and moderation.

PEONIES

THE PEONY BLOSSOMS ALWAYS NEEDED SHAKING OFF AFTER A rainstorm. Weighted with water, they had to be helped to stand straight and proud once again, so their petals were transformed from soggy, crumpled blobs to shimmering, floating organdy ballet skirts once more.

The emancipation project took only a few minutes, because my mother wasn't one to go overboard with peonies. Certainly she liked their frilly, pastel-colored blossoms well enough; that much was clear from the number of them tumbling from vases on the kitchen table. But in her infinite wisdom (unequivocal in such matters, but not necessarily equally so concerning the selection of comfortable play clothes), she knew that peonies are best taken in small doses.

A few peonies integrated into the garden worked just fine. They romped around with everything else in perfect harmony, no better or worse than the roses, geraniums, irises, lady's mantle, and everything else that bloomed at the same time. A peony here and there in the garden was perfectly delightful; it was so essential a component, in

fact, that you didn't mind wading through the centaurea or brushing past the shoulder-high nepeta just to shake off the flower heads after a rainstorm.

But when peonies began to run as a herd, they changed personality entirely. Get too many together, and pretty soon they were a white-glove affair. As soon as that happened, you were forced to put on scratchy crinoline, spotless white anklets, and freshly shined Mary Janes just to be in their presence. Suddenly, instead of tumbling around the place in a spirited game of king of the mountain, you were forced to wait your turn patiently in a lethargic round of croquet. Peonies were just like parents: when you got them together, their sense of humor vanished completely.

It was obvious why the peonies beside the croquet lawn at posh resort hotels had to be staked while their compatriots in the garden were allowed to go lax. It was perfectly understandable why every branch beside the croquet pitch required a crutch to support the weight of its flowers against the winds that blew over the adjacent immaculately manicured lawn. Those peonies – the headstrong and opinionated ones, the ones that always stood on ceremony and were too good to wallow with forget-me-nots and similar ragamuffins – hadn't yet befriended a little girl. They hung around solely with adults – and with other peonies, which is never a good idea.

ROSES

ON WARM EARLY-SUMMER AFTERNOONS WHEN THE SUN WAS still gentle enough for us to bask safely in its beams, we sat on the front porch after lunch while my mother read aloud. That was when I first heard *A Child's Garden of Verses* and *Poems for Little Ears*. Much later on, at bedtime, my father read *Winnie-the-Pooh* and *The Wind in the Willows* by the nightlight beside our beds. But noon was the province of poetry.

Most of the time I would doze off. By the time we were well into "My Shadow" and "The Lamplighter," I was drifting away in my mother's lap. But the yellow rose that climbed up the pillars of the porch must have received quite an education. By early summer, when it was full of plump maize-colored buds, the poetry readings were in

MAKING ROSE POTPOURRI

Snag rose petals for drying before they shatter and fall to the ground. Harvest roses on a dry day, following several dry days, when the flowers are in their prime. Immediately set to work at the painstaking task of pulling the tissue-thin, easily shredded and bruised petals from the greenery. Spread the petals out on newspaper or a flat screen so they scarcely overlap and stash them in a dark, well-ventilated place, like the attic. When the petals are light and crisp, mix them thoroughly with a heaping tablespoon of ground fixative, such as calamus root or sliced orris, adding a heaping tablespoon of fixative for each quart of dried ingredients. Then add a few drops of rose or rose geranium oil for scent and close them in containers to be opened later.

full swing. I have happy memories of the yellow rose – of sitting in its shadow, drinking in its musky scent, watching sleepily as spent silken petals fluttered lazily to the ground. The rose and I got along just fine from a distance.

Intimacy did not warm the relationship. In later years, when a chair of my own and *Treasure Island* replaced the time once devoted to being read to and the rose had stretched its way up to the eaves, I decided it was my duty to save it from Japanese beetles. That summer those pests reached plague proportions, and every beetle in the country headed straight for our yellow climbing rose. They gnawed on its foliage until only the leaf skeletons remained, and they chewed on the blossoms until nothing was left but a Swiss cheese of brown holes. They hid in the buds and hollowed out their hearts, leaving only the façade.

I came to the rescue. From the outset, it was a nasty business, pulling all those ugly beetles from the branches and crushing them into a disgusting paste. But the worst of it was the rose. You have never met a less grateful shrub in your life. My skirmishes with the neighborhood boys and with my sisters were nothing compared to the battle I waged with that miserable rose while trying to free it from bugs. It impaled me, tore my sleeves, and ripped my blouse. It added injury to insult, snagging my hair in its briars and refusing to let go. The more I struggled, the more tightly it wound my hair (unruly at the best of times) around itself. It wasn't long before I concluded that the Japanese beetles were just a minor annoyance compared to the rose itself.

And the situation grew worse. As the years passed, the rose reached greater heights, but I failed to grow with equal speed. It became even more beautiful, its blossoms providing even more reasons to defend it from aggressors. But now I had to perform the task balanced on a stepladder while trying both to grab the beetles and to grapple with the thorny, vine-enwrapped pillar for support. Although the rose carried its beetle-lure aloft, its artillery went the entire length of its branches; I invariably emerged from the scene looking as if I'd been involved in a street brawl. And lost.

I never reached a truce with the rose. But it taught me something about beauty, and what lies beneath.

FLOWER GARLANDS

A LITTLE GIRL DOESN'T NEED AN EXCUSE TO WEAR A CROWN of flowers. And once I had one on my head, nothing could make me take it off – not even playing red rover or mother-may-I.

The first garland I remember was woven of nothing more self-important than dandelions, their juicy stems linked together in loose sailor's knots, their golden blossoms glowing in the twilight as I counted backward in the shrubbery during a spirited game of hide-and-seek.

MAKING A GARLAND

Airy flowers with many blooms on a stem work best in garlands, so lady's mantle, goldenrod, and baby's breath are veterans. Long stems are essential, because the stems are linked, one to the next, as in a relay race. Join them together with string, thread, or light-gauge wire. Begin by taking a cluster of three- or four-blossom stems and wrapping the wire (or whatever you're using) around them. Then add another bunch just below the first, extending the garland with it and wrapping it in with the wire. When you have a chain of the proper length for a crown, make a circle by tying together the wire at both ends. To keep the garland moist until it's worn, float it in a shallow bowl of water, but remember to shake off the excess moisture before putting it on.

This makeshift garland was responsible for leaving a telltale trail of petals and stems when it was my turn to hide, since I ran as fast as possible to be engulfed in the denseness of the hydrangea's branches while a friend counted from behind the hedge (skipping several numbers and never giving me enough time to disappear entirely).

But that wasn't a deterrent to wearing garlands. They didn't survive a barn dance or a cousin's wedding either. Despite the fact that they were always askew, forever falling into my eyes, usually half wilted, I usually had one balanced on my head. My mother encouraged this obsession. Of course, it was entirely possible that she had improved posture as a motive, or an effective disguise for the kinks of hair continually standing on end. She was always willing to sacrifice some garden flowers for a little fantasy and a clumsy crown.

Some mothers could make bona fide flower crowns. I was in a ballet recital once with a girl whose mother wove a confection of many blossoms specifically for the occasion. You could immediately discern the quality of the goods. This crown was like an entire garden distilled into a strand of flowers. It was the stuff of princesses and fancy dress balls and brought to mind royalty as well as romance.

That girl, who was not particularly well coordinated or light on her feet, was transformed when she donned the garland. She suddenly became a prima ballerina in our eyes. She didn't fidget; she didn't fling herself around. Instead, she stepped into the role of queen and became lovely beyond imagination. It doesn't really matter how homely or awkward you were before you put on a garland of flowers – you become beautiful. Flower garlands can do that for you.

DELPHINIUMS

SOME FLOWERS REMAINED THE STUFF OF DREAMS — DELPHINIUMS, for example. No one in our neighborhood could successfully convince delphiniums to survive for several consecutive years. Even if you whined and nagged at the garden center until your mother finally agreed to purchase a few, no one had the patience to stake them strongly enough to withstand the winds that buffeted the spot where they could be displayed to best advantage. Like Lassie, they looked good from a distance. But who wanted to keep such a beast trained, groomed, and exercised?

Instead, we encountered delphiniums on vacation. While driving up through coastal Maine and winding along poorly paved, bumpy roads where we were all told to keep our eyes peeled for the motel (which didn't take much urging, considering how hungry we were, despite all the Tootsie Rolls handed out along the way) – that's when we met these stately flowers.

Delphiniums were always admired from a distance. They were the tall spires of fantasy – forbidden fruit, so to speak. And they were fantastic. Where they deigned to thrive, they multiplied with such a flourish and in such outrageous numbers that a double-take was always necessary, despite the fact that we were all concentrating on visions of Howard Johnson's chicken pot pie. Delphiniums were like Oz, an Emerald City of dense plumes and poker-straight stems that didn't topple despite the ocean breezes. Nothing could be further from the delphiniums in my mother's garden, which fell over before the flowers opened and suffered from blight, threatening certain doom.

Even when I saw the flowers close up, great foxtail-like spires for sale at a farmstand where we stopped to pick up peaches to quell our mounting hunger, they didn't look real. First of all, the color resembled nothing found in our back yard, or anywhere in our neighborhood. These delphiniums bristled in a strange, untrustworthy blue that defied reality. Furthermore, they were in the habit of brandishing several surreal shades, like the aquamarine at the bottom of the pool, porcelain pink, the purest snow-driven white, and so on.

It wasn't only the color range that moved them safely into the realm of mirage. Have you ever seen such a complex flower on any other plant? Someone once pointed out that every individual delphinium

GROWING DELPHINIUMS

If delphiniums survive, you can thank mulch. The secret to delphiniums lies in keeping the roots moist and cool in summer and protected from freezing and thawing in winter. It's done with mulch, laid thickly and applied early in the plants' life. Delphiniums dislike summer heat, which explains why they thrive along shorelines, despite the brisk winds. To counteract gusts, stake the tall, top-heavy flower stalks as soon as they start to stretch skyward. To improve the chances of a perennial performance, you can remove all the flower stalks in the initial growing season. But that's a difficult task when you know that delphiniums aren't always reliably perennial.

flower holds what looks like a bee trapped in its center. Sure enough, when I looked, it seemed that an insect was indeed caught in the middle of those strangely colored petals. But that was just half of it. Upon closer examination, the flower gained more ruffles and frills than good taste usually permitted. A spire in full glory held dozens of blossoms, all equally overdressed for the occasion. One thing was clear: whoever created delphiniums obviously had a darn good time in the process.

That's what delphiniums were all about. They were the flowers that proclaimed that the limits of creativity could be stretched. Although they were the phantoms of the garden, always slightly beyond reach and existing only somewhere else, they opened a door. Like a circus act or a carnival scene, they lit your imagination and let it roam. If such a flower could come into being, anything was possible.

TEA PARTIES

SUMMER HAD A WAY OF WEARING ON YOU. AT FIRST IT WAS all outings and excitement – watching seeds sprout, making mud pies. But eventually you wearied of all the commotion, and even the mud pies failed to hold your attention. When you had pestered everyone ad nauseam with endless pointed hints about ponies without seeing anything remotely like a horse materialize in the back yard, it was time to seek new diversions.

The beauty of living in a close-knit neighborhood where everyone pretty much knew everyone else's business was that you could go and spy on other people's gardens. When I tired of all the usual summer activities – when I'd swung until I was dizzy and hidden in all the obvious hiding places without having anyone really hunt me up – I began to check out other people's back yards.

From the shrubbery, it was possible to monitor discreetly what was going on in our neighbors' flowerbeds (if they didn't have a dog) on any given day. I knew with fair accuracy whose sweet peas had sprouted first and who had planted their sweet peas so late that the hot weather curtailed the crop. I knew that the Phillipses had fallen head over heels for tea roses and that the Emersons were up to their eyeballs in summer squash. A better child might have offered to take some of the harvest off their hands, but I wasn't that sort of kid.

For better or worse, such neighborhoods are often strictly divided by age group. For the most part, I played with kids who lived nearby and were approximately my own age. Part of the education I got in summer had to do with watching other kids play. From my vantage point, I could keep tabs on what was going on with the eight-year-old segment of society, for example. And some of the reconnaissance proved useful.

Other little girls held tea parties. The sisters down the street, for example, indulged on a regular basis. They wore clean starched frocks just begging to be stained, laid a table with their mother's delicate demitasse service (for some reason she entrusted them with it), and dragged out every doll they could find, propping each one up on a scaled-down wooden chair. They poured apple juice while precariously balancing on their mother's high heels, clinked the fine bone china, wiped their lips with lace handkerchiefs, and nibbled on store-bought

cookies while wearing oversize sunbonnets. From my vantage point behind a hedge, it wasn't my sort of affair.

Sometimes you can take an idea and define it in your own terms, and that's what happened with tea parties. There were some intriguing concepts there, like dolls and cookies. We didn't have a miniature tea set, but there were plenty of small cups and saucers that had been wounded in action during dishwashing catastrophes. We didn't have much in the way of down-scaled furniture, except for a child-size collapsible chair that was convenient for lawn concerts. But I could use the lawn chairs.

You have to develop your own take on tea parties. They should challenge your creativity, especially as you make centerpieces or arrangements at the individual place settings (if you feel the urge). No etiquette whatsoever should be inflicted, and no table manners should be instilled. Yelling is encouraged. Comfortable attire should be worn – no high heels. Grass stains must prevail. There should be plenty of crumbs. Ideally, a tea party should reflect all your penchants and include all the things you hold dear, like the cats and feathered friends.

BEYOND IMAGINATION

PARENTS ARE FOND OF EXPEDITIONS. THEY LIKE TO PACK a picnic lunch, load you into the car, and fill the glove compartment with bags of M&M's (which lasted longer before meltdown than chocolate kisses), crayons, paper, dot-to-dot games, and other bribes to keep the peace. On any given Sunday, we'd be bound somewhere. Sunday drives with no fixed destination were the worst scenarios. When my mother actually unfolded a map – proof beyond doubt that a goal had been set – an audible sigh of relief could be heard from the back seat.

I wasn't the best traveler in the family. I was the first to ask if we were lost yet as we rolled up and down hills. By the time we arrived at our destination, I was a wreck. So, by extension, were my parents. Tired, disheveled, and cranky, I would fall out of the back seat, my dress rumpled, my face smeared with candy, and proceed to make museumgoing miserable for everyone who had the misfortune of being in our audio-guided tour. It is a testimony to my mother's fortitude that she continued in the pursuit of culture despite my efforts to dissuade her

from seeing anything more than fifteen minutes away from home.

But one excursion was different. It stays firmly in a memory that has successfully blotted out all the Van Goghs, Monets, and Sargents that undoubtedly crossed my path during my formative years. I remember an expedition that entailed many miserable hours along winding roads. I remember threatening to get sick if the car wasn't halted immediately, and I remember making gagging noises to prove my point. More clearly, I recall finally pulling into a long allée of trees and sensing that something different was in store.

A pair of gigantic peacocks, probably done in yew, flanked the path to the bathroom, which, according to tradition, was our first port of call. After that, it was all just a blur of billowing borders dense with plants that stood taller and plumper than all of us. There was a magnitude of scope, design, color, intent, and intensity. Surely it was a fantasy world, and yet that fantasy stretched quite tangibly before our eyes. I could see, touch, and smell it. It was perplexing and seductive in the same breath.

I recall statues stretching up to the sky, their sleek marble cool to the touch. Long, rolling deer parks led to ponds that reflected pavilions beside weeping willows on distant shores. Borders were packed with plants and flowers, and gardens were filled just with roses, delphiniums, or irises – dozens of them, perhaps even hundreds, all together in one garden. Everything was larger than life. It was another world entirely.

Of course, we had flowers around the foundation of our house. There was a modest garden in the yard, devoted to whatever caught my mother's fancy each year. Although the foundation beds undulated slightly to skirt the arborvitae, soldier-straight lines were the norm. As far as garden ornaments went, we had a birdbath for a while, but my sisters and I succeeded in breaking it when we had a relay race from the back door, down the slide, around my mother's little nod to garden ornamentation, and into the inflated pool.

The inflated pool, which was undeniably refreshing, in no way compared to the rippling ponds in the public garden I visited that day. And the birdbath, riveting though it may have been for a few minutes after it was installed by my father, was nothing compared to the fountains with their tiers of dolphins, mermaids, and sea nymphs. This was a world dense with exotic flowering shrubs and strange trees. Instead

of raised ranch houses and split-levels, there were glass houses with weird vines climbing out of the ventilators. Men of few words wearing soiled overalls wheeled barrows and clipped away with a fervor and confidence that defied anyone to distract them.

It took me no time at all to lose my parents and sisters entirely. I was crouched over a baby's tears, patting it, when a pair of muddy boots came into my field of vision. The gardener was leaning on a hoe, and I recall looking up as he asked if I knew the name of the plant at my feet. I didn't answer, because he was, after all, a stranger. But he told me that it was baby's tears, the same as I cried. I hadn't seen my parents or sisters for what was certainly several minutes; I didn't have my sweater with me, and my family was apparently on the verge of calling out the local authorities for a statewide search. But at the time, crying was the last thing on my mind.

H O L L Y H O C K S

SUMMER DIDN'T TRULY HIT ITS STRIDE UNTIL THE HOLLYHOCKS opened. Not really. Before the hollyhocks, there might be fireflies and cloudbursts, heat waves and sleep-outs, but they flitted by like the cabbage moths that hovered over the garden. They failed to linger in your mind's eye. But the hollyhocks stuck. Thumb through all the summers you remember and all the summers you've nearly forgotten, and chances are that hollyhocks will still stand tall.

Hollyhocks were the synthesis of summer. First of all, they took forever to open. After all the precocious little overachievers of early summer had burst on the scene and petered out, the hollyhocks were still gathering steam. There is something to be said for the building of suspense, and hollyhocks had drama.

They also possessed an element of absurdity that you couldn't help but value when you'd just finished reading half a dozen Nancy Drew mysteries in two weeks' time. There was nothing prissy about holly-hocks. Shooting up higher than you remembered from previous years, they were the gangly behemoths of the garden.

No matter how tall you grew, the hollyhocks grew taller. Eventually, they towered over the rest of creation. But then, on top of their ridiculously spindly spires, they balanced blossoms – blossoms of indescribable colors. Their luminous buds opened in shades that don't exist in crayon boxes or fingerpaints, hues you'd never seen before, in combinations that couldn't be duplicated.

It wasn't only the colors. Hollyhocks had movement. They danced. They got into such a frenzy, in fact, that they usually ended up toppling in a heap on the ground. And that, to my mind, was their most laudable quality. No matter how many stakes my mother hauled to the garden, no matter how many times she went out and bound flower spikes to bamboo, the hollyhocks always broke loose. There really was no disciplining them. They evaded all attempts at containment, and they danced. They swayed in the breeze, and when things began to heat up and lightning flashed and the electricity blew, they all swung with their bamboo poles until something snapped.

My mother went out the next morning before the breakfast dishes were done, with a scowl and her apron still on, and tried to restore order. She attempted to disentangle the hollyhocks, which lay on the ground in a pile from the tango the night before. She muttered; she sorted the mess; she leaned each spire back against the fence and tied it with twine. In effect, she sent each of them to its own room. But it did no good. Two days later, there they'd be again, in a monstrous brawl on the grass. And that's what you remember most about hollyhocks – not only that they tower, but that they fall. Hang the consequences, forget the inevitable outcome; hollyhocks just know how to have fun.

LANTERNS AND LILIES

YOU REMEMBER MIDSUMMER NIGHTS. THEY WERE LONG AND languid, steamy, sticky, and conducive to tossing and turning. They provided an opportunity for strange dreams to visit, dreams that sent you out onto the front porch to find your parents. And there they were, rocking and talking, with cool drinks at their sides and a thin light coming through the window from the kitchen. On midsummer nights, the neighborhood sounds floated through your windows until the darkness was thick with dogs barking, cats serenading, raccoons squabbling, owls courting, a piano playing. That music mixed with the relentless drone of crickets, katydids, and frogs to form the symphony of midsummer. Distant thunder rolled, heat lightning flashed, and

MAKING HOLLYHOCK DOLLS

Hollyhock dolls require little in the way of supplies. Obviously, you need hollyhock flowers; an assortment of different colors is ideal. A few unopened buds are also helpful. Then you're in business. Nip off the stem of the calyx (the green part that attaches the petals together), slip in a toothpick, and voilà! The open flowers serve as skirts and petticoats while the buds are the heads. The dolls can wear hats or sport outrageous hairdos (withered flowers make great coiffures). If you stick a toothpick sideways across the first one and attach flowers on both sides, you've got sleeves.

fireflies floated up and down, up and down, like yo-yos in a meadow. If you inhaled, the scent was dense with nicotianas, tuberoses, and lilies. More than anything, the lilies defined those sultry nights.

When you're very young, the world isn't limited by the boundaries of reality. Show a little girl a picture of lanterns in a moonlit garden, and forever after (or at least while her imagination holds sway) midsummer nights will be the realm of lilies and lantern light. Pretty soon she'll be telling stories of lanterns floating in the twilight, describing the way the slightest breeze sent them dancing and the flame swelled their bellies and defined the splints that made their sides. Her cheeks will flush as she spins the scene. When a little girl is captivated by an idea, she makes it her own. She embroiders it and tailors it until midsummer evenings always belong to lanterns and lilies.

That's the way with midsummer magic. Such a profusion dominates summer as the days slip into each other, with everything blossoming simultaneously, that it's difficult to discriminate. The garden becomes like a crowded city street, with so many pedestrians that you don't see individual faces anymore. Then there's night, and the protagonists stand out.

Although the lilies were mildly intriguing by day, they beguiled the dark. When leaves and branches disappeared into shadows, trees were silhouetted eerily, and all the creatures of the night came out, the garden was recast. Then the lilies stepped into the spotlight, their giant blossoms dancing like a constellation of stars. Their perfume intoxicated the air, and their flowers gained depth and character. But mostly they became the fodder of fantasy, the stardust of dreams. Because when you show a little girl a picture of lanterns and lilies, then lilies will never be the same. And midsummer nights will also be transformed.

CHAPTER FOUR

AUTUMN

HERE IS NEVER TIME TO MOURN THE LOSS OF summer, because autumn rushes in too quickly for regrets. In fact, autumn comes and goes with a speed that is rivaled only by the pace of a scooter racing downhill. Its crisp days slipped through your fingers – one day the world was immersed in festive zinnias and morning glories, and the next it was suddenly swamped in fiery fallen leaves. There is scarcely enough time to plan a route to school that will pass both the Shetland pony and the candy store before we have to decide what to wear for Halloween.

Autumn is an odyssey that begins with one foot in summer but the other poised to leap headlong into wool sweaters, bonfires, and cider. Everything begins to change. No matter how many failures you've experienced during the past growing season, they no longer matter. In autumn, everything is forgiven. With the wisdom gained from that knowledge, the world becomes more brilliant. Autumn has a vividness, a determination to move forward, to blow out the dust from the corners and make the garden anew. You become an explorer in the promised land – along with your mother, of course.

HYDRANGEAS

THE HEAVY CLOUDS OF HYDRANGEA BLOSSOMS MEANT THAT pretty soon we would be dressed up in brand-new clothes and packed onto Velveeta-colored buses to begin another stretch in school. As surely as sweet peas signaled the start of vacation and roses marked the time when you could kick off your shoes and run barefoot on fresh green grass, hydrangeas marked the end of summer. To anyone who wasn't burdened by multiplication tables and long division, hydrangeas were probably a welcome sight. But for me, they meant the gradual disappearance of afternoons dedicated to nothing more mentally taxing than collecting bugs for the insect jar and feeding the ducks at Washington Crossing State Park.

Hydrangeas weren't really the end of the affair. Summer still had some mileage, but you had to move swiftly to get all your loafing accomplished before the schoolbuses started lumbering along their

DRYING HYDRANGEAS

Wait until the blossoms turn from soft and supple to dry and papery to cut hydrangeas for drying. If you cut them when they are too moist, the flowers will shrivel. Handle them gingerly. Hydrangea branches are brittle and prone to snap (decapitate would be a better word, because they invariably break just below the head) with no provocation at all. The most efficient method of drying is to bunch the flowers, tie them with a rubber band, and hang them upside down for two to three weeks in a well-ventilated, dark place. The darkness is crucial for preserving the color. When fully dried, they can go into vases with no water, and they'll last a year or more in perfect condition. However, even after they've dried, hydrangeas are fragile, and they leave a telltale trail of litter when they're moved.

daily routes. For that purpose, hydrangeas filled the bill, because there was no better secret hiding place than a hydrangea shrub in full flower.

Every child has a hiding place. Some are more elaborate than others, but every kid needs a spot to disappear to at opportune moments. I had several, and I spent a lot of time hidden in them, especially when my mother was on the rampage to remind me to practice something or other.

Other kids built hiding places, which sort of defeated the purpose, given the amount of noise that accompanied the accumulation of old wood planks, and other debris. When the time came to clean up your room, you certainly didn't want the world to know where you'd chosen to go undercover. If you were the kind of child who needed a swank bungalow, that was one thing. But most of us were perfectly content with a snug piece of soft ground and complete privacy.

The weeping willow was also a wonderful refuge. The fact that the massive old tree committed several crimes and misdemeanors, such as breaking and entering the sewer lines in search of moisture, didn't bother me at all. Loyalty was a more important trait. The tree spilled a shower of branches right to the ground, ensuring that no one was likely to discover a fugitive concealed under its skirts. The willow never betrayed my confidence.

The hollowed-out center of the spirea under the kitchen window – a spot I appropriated from Shadow, the cat – was also a prime hiding place. It had the disadvantage of being cramped, though, especially when shared with Shadow. The hydrangea, in contrast, was spacious and possessed all the qualities you need in a retreat. Not only was it dense, but enough dappled light penetrated to allow reading without eyestrain. If it occurred to anyone that the time I spent hidden there was probably every bit as valuable as the hours I devoted to Dick and Jane at school, she never said so. As a learning facility, the hydrangea got no credit whatsoever.

The day inevitably came when I was forced out of concealment, not without protest. When no daylight hours remained after dinner to go outside and play and I had to put on a sweater after snacks, I was in trouble. But the most telling sign that school was looming came when my mother sheared the hydrangea of its big, fat flower trusses so she could bring them inside to dry.

DAHLIAS

FOR THE MOST PART, MY MOTHER GREW A GARDEN OF NO-nonsense flowers. Usually she showed a definite preference for roses, irises, lilies, and that sort of sedate thing. As I recall, the colors were subdued. By and large, everything fit comfortably into the realm of good taste; there was nothing shocking, and decorum reigned in our back yard. Except for a few dahlias.

Think about it. Can you remember exactly what the peonies looked like in the gardens of your youth? Can you summon the precise hue in the irises that grew on the edge of the pond or the roses that clambered on the wall or fence? I can't. I can't recall the specific color of any of my mother's roses, with the exception of the yellow climber that eavesdropped on the front porch. But I do remember the dahlias.

Something about the dahlias came within footsteps of the surreal. To be sure, they have a "look at me" attitude. But it's more than that. Dahlias could easily audition for a science-fiction movie and capture the roles of the space aliens. For that matter, a dahlia could be the understudy for Godzilla, or at least play the star attraction in Godzilla's garden.

For all these reasons and because they are notoriously unpredictable as far as their color scheme is concerned, dahlias didn't assume a leading part in our back yard. I was fascinated by the few we had, though, and assumed that my mother put them there herself – they hadn't escaped from the zoo or wandered into her realm by other accidental means. That realization made me think there were facets of my mother that I didn't know at all. She wore her hair in a conservative cut. She dressed in whatever slender fitted suit happened to be in vogue. Our living room looked very much like all the rest in the neighborhood. But there were those dahlias in the yard, doing all sorts of insane things.

They weren't particularly attractive plants. A lot of the time, they mimicked salad greens. Often you wandered into the garden after watching all the TV you possibly could in a single sitting, and the dahlias were just a big, dull blob of beefy leaves brandishing buds in suspended animation. But then one day they opened. On a day when you'd fidgeted over your Cheerios for so long that your mother sent you outside to play in order to regain her mental balance and wipe up the spills from the kitchen floor, you headed for the dahlias and discovered things that looked like gigantic sea urchins.

GROWING DAHLIAS

Dahlias need warmth, and so they have to be planted when danger of frost is past. Wait until you can sift the earth through your fingers comfortably and it's neither warm nor cold. Then the dahlia tubers can come out of the cellar (or the store) and go into the garden. Plant them six inches deep if you don't want to hill them up, three inches deep if you're willing to mound soil around their stems after they've sprouted. No supplemental water is necessary immediately after planting, but they're thirsty when growth becomes robust and especially when the buds begin to swell – which happens toward late summer, after an excruciatingly long wait. When frost has curtailed the show, dig the tubers, dry them for a few hours, and pack them in a crate of peat moss in the cellar until next spring.

Have you ever noticed that a dahlia changes as it unfolds – that one day it looks like an anemone and a few days later it mimics a rose? The flowers change colors as well. As they develop, nuances are revealed. Suddenly a tarty-looking flower becomes something of a fashion plate. Every dahlia is an artist at heart, and I figure that's the sort of free-spirited expression my mother wanted to cultivate. She wanted to expose us to the renegade zeal of a flower with pluck, passion, and a modicum of grace. She wanted us to experience dissidence. To a degree.

If ever there were flowers begging to be cut, it was the dahlias. Messing around in the roses was such an unpleasant business that no one had to reel off the list of punishments that would result if I swiped a few blossoms. The same held for most of the other flowers around the house. But the dahlias were another matter entirely.

Of course, now I wonder if my mother didn't plant the dahlias just so we would pick them. It's possible that she indulged in them partly because she knew that one day we'd wander over and interact. She might have planted those dahlias to lead us into cutting a few and playing with flowers that had spunk, color, and minds of their own. She might have planted them because the blossoms could be fiddled with for a while before wilting, or because they were good to cut, or maybe just because they were different.

MORNING GLORIES

I NEVER WOKE UP BEFORE THE MORNING GLORIES. BY THE TIME I'd finished breakfast and fed the dog, turtles, canary, and goldfish, that day's crop of heavenly blue trumpets was nearly on the verge of waning. By the time the day had warmed into a blush of heat and the sun had worked itself into sweltering, the flowers were long gone. Morning glories saw the best of the day.

They were also filled with trust. Most flowers seemed to lack foresight. Take the poppies, for example: dawn came and went and the day reached adolescence before they fully opened. Promises weren't enough for them; they required proof that the sun would kiss their petals. Poppies didn't take risks. But morning glories were prone to leaps of faith. They began acting their part in the scene before the daily curtain cracked open. Before dawn was announced and the mourning doves cooed, the morning glories were there, waiting.

And they played a pivotal role. Everything in the garden served a function: the roses prevented anyone, good or bad, from entering the front door without being frisked; the spirea provided a hiding spot where I could crouch and concentrate on reading *Champion Dog Prince Tom* uninterrupted. And if it weren't for morning glories, the neighbors' prying eyes would be peering directly at us.

Of course, in the beginning of the summer, when the soil was still too chilly for the morning glories, we were exposed to public scrutiny. Everyone who passed could see that all of last winter's leaves hadn't been raked away and the cat had scratched out half the sempervivens and left them strewn on the patio. So my mother hastily planted the morning glories, soaking the seeds for a day or two to give them a good head start. She didn't want to leave such things to chance.

GROWING MORNING GLORIES

Most often, morning glories just reappear. Once they're planted, you can expect them year after year, even though they're not perennial – the seeds just sow themselves in. If they don't come up voluntarily, or if you need morning glories of a different color, soak the seeds for a day or two in water before planting them an inch below the soil surface. (However, morning glory seeds are poisonous – this is not a project for young children.) Choose a place with lean soil that isn't overburdened with abundant compost. Morning glories aren't hungry, but they are thirsty plants. Since the foliage wilts easily and the flowers fold when the sun is bright, plant them on the east or west side of a building or fence so they get some shade. When they finish blooming, leave the vines in place to ensure another year of self-sown seeds.

Once they had sprouted, the vines got right down to the serious business at hand. While we were giving the yard its summer weeding and straightening up, the morning glories stepped in to hide all the remaining blemishes from public view. No one realized that behind the screen of glistening blue blossoms that greeted dawn but grew weary by the time we came home from school, there were weeds in the beds and mildew on the phlox.

Thanks to the morning glories, I formed a pact with my mother. While my father was at work and other mothers were strolling by with their baby carriages, my mother and I hid away in our garden. It wasn't as perfect as other gardens on earth; it wasn't symmetrical or filled with bed after bed of alyssum. But it was our place, and we found fascination there.

I was aware that my mother wore neither lipstick nor high heels when she gardened, but the neighbors never knew. If the pocket of her dress caught on a thorn and ripped or she got smudges on her knees from kneeling, she didn't bother to go inside and change. Not after the morning glories began to blossom, anyway.

I figured that you had to get up early in the morning to keep such a fundamental trust. After all, you never knew when someone would have to rush outside, curlers still in her hair, cold cream still on her forehead, to retrieve a newspaper. On such occasions, my mother didn't hesitate before racing out in her robe and slippers, because she knew the morning glories would be there. Ready.

ZINNIAS

WE GREW ZINNIAS BECAUSE THE LIONS' FAIR, THE BIG Apple Circus, and the Rotary Club Carnival couldn't last forever, a carpet of slimy algae eventually covered the pond, and the big kids took over the rope swing at the lake. Zinnias were there because we even got bored with running back and forth through the sprinkler, screaming bloody murder.

We didn't have scads of these fiesta-colored flowers. In fact, I've always suspected that my mother grew the zinnias specifically to decorate the lemonade stand. When she finished sweeping up the last insect liberated from the ant farm and caught the finch that escaped when

FRESH
BOUQUETS
$ 5.⁰⁰

ZINNIA
BOUQUETS
$5.⁰⁰

CABBAGE
49

SOWING ZINNIAS

Zinnias are ideal candidates for a sowing project. Vying with marigolds as the simplest seeds to sow, they are apt to sprout faster than most children will lose interest, and they are capable of withstanding some manhandling during transplanting. Plant them close together in a small herd, spacing each plant eighteen to twenty-four inches from its brethren. Watering is the secret to getting zinnia flowers and lots of them. Water the plants early in the summer to give them a vigorous start. Also, pluck out the growing tip of the central stem early in the game to encourage branching. Inevitably, a glut of flowers will be produced, more than you can possibly harvest for lemonade stands, which makes deadheading essential.

someone left the cage door open, she tactfully suggested a lemonade stand.

This was a truly welcome diversion, certainly head and shoulders above sweeping the patio or cleaning the dog run. The lemonade itself fell under my mother's jurisdiction. I was responsible for the zinnias.

The most difficult part was deciding which colors could be spared. My mother insisted that zinnias produced more blossoms when the flowers were cut, but the fact is that eight-year-olds do not live for the future. For a child, tomorrow has no bearing whatever in the balance of a zinnia equation. At the moment of truth, every one of those flowers wanted to stay in the garden. They all preferred to stretch their stems up to the bathroom window, furnishing companionship on the other side of the pane while I splashed in the tub.

If the future was factored in, tomorrow's inherent unpredictability colored the decision-making process. Who could promise that later flowers would bear the same brilliant shade of orange? Who could say for sure that future zinnias would have as many petals so neatly stacked one on top of the next? It might rain for the next five weeks, so there were no flowers whatsoever. Or it might never rain again, with equally dire consequences. Scraping up enough zinnias for the lemonade stand was full of painful dilemmas.

Of course, by the time I had weighed the merits of each blossom and gathered all the necessary jars, tins, and Coke bottles, all the fathers in the neighborhood had already driven by on their way home from work. When the signs were finally crayoned and I'd successfully smudged my clothes with indelible Magic Marker, it was usually time to wash up for dinner.

LAVENDER AND LINENS

No MATTER HOW HECTIC THE REST OF THE WORLD BECAME, how many bullies tormented me on the school bus, or how much trouble I had memorizing the three times table, my grandmother's house was a haven of calm. From the moment we rang the bell and she threw open the front door to scoop me up into a big soft hug, the pace slowed to a steady, sweet, syrupy rhythm in which nothing remarkable occurred but nothing bad ever happened either. And everything tasted delicious.

No one ran around in my grandmother's house, tearing through the rooms and rattling the china in the cabinet. Instead, it was a place for sinking into cushy chairs and snoozing to the monotones of adults talking, sometimes in a language that I couldn't understand. Every once in a while my name would come up and all the relatives would look over and beam, and that's how I would know that the conversation had turned to the spelling bee I'd won the previous week or something similar. The rest of the conversation seemed equally benevolent.

In my grandmother's house, there was white linen everywhere, with crocheted edges, pressed and starched and laid on the arms of the chairs, on the sideboard, beside the bathroom sink, straddling the chair backs. Handwoven dish towels were folded beside the kitchen sink, their nubby texture soft from many, many washings. And the entire house was infused with the scent of lavender. There was nothing brash or disturbing to your nose, just the steady scent of lavender, like a ticking clock. The whole place had a prevailing full-bodied perfume, slightly musky but very clean.

The scent had nothing to do with the garden, and it wasn't confined to summer. Its source, first discovered during an afternoon's scavenger hunt, was the huge mahogany wardrobe where the linens were folded, waiting for company to arrive. Long ago the aroma had escaped from behind those closed doors to permeate the house. Just barely perceptible, lurking faintly in corners, becoming stronger when you buried your face in a pillow, was the scent of lavender. Wherever my grandmother moved, the scent would follow. That much you could depend on.

The lavender lulled us to sleep. At the end of the day, we sank onto sheets that had fluttered on the line until they were dry and we reeled

them in to be liberated from their clothespins. We took them off, shook them out with a brisk flap (just to show them who was in charge), and performed the little folding dance that is passed down through the generations of mothers and daughters, the choreography of walking forward, meeting, touching corners, relaying folds, stooping to retrieve the dangling ends, and walking forward with them again. Sometimes I watched while the sheets were ironed with lavender water, which sat in a bowl by the ironing board and which my grandmother sent flying with a quick shake of her fingertips to christen the fabric. Always sachets of dried lavender were tucked into the folds before the sheets were stacked in the linen cabinet.

I recall the sweet taste of my favorite chocolate pudding as it came steaming out of my grandmother's oven and the sound of her poorly tuned, tinny piano being played as we nodded off to sleep at night, but it's the scent of lavender that lingers most steadfastly. Wherever I encounter it, it delivers me right back to my grandmother's house.

LAST FLOWERS

IF YOU LISTENED TO MY MOTHER, EVERY CLOSED GATE SECRETED a garden. Hidden behind every barricade was a flower-laden landscape waiting to be discovered. This was an intriguing concept. But as far as trick-or-treating was concerned, it had definite disadvantages. Not only did you have to worry about dogs and other ferocious creatures (I've known roosters that would make a pit bull look tame), but you had to steer around the autumn flowers that might be stashed behind all those garden gates.

It was my considered opinion that gardens impeded the serious business of trick-or-treating. Because you normally went out in your costume after dark, you were forced to stumble over all the asters and chrysanthemums that people put in awkward places when the rest of the garden had slipped away. Leave the front yard open to pedestrian traffic and clear for collecting candy, that was my line. Hasten the garden to bed. Bedraggled and brittle, prone to break at the least provocation, autumn flowers were best left by the roadside, where they belonged.

Don't misunderstand: I wouldn't begrudge the season its last gasp for the world. It was a delightfully melancholy moment. Autumn accentuated the closeness in our family as we gathered around and turned our attention to building complicated rocket models, and it simultaneously brought out all my mother's deeply buried tendencies to squirrel.

The season had a wonderfully unstudied quality. It was a time of scraps. We took many walks, trying to wedge in a few last treks before everything disappeared, first under leaves, then under snow. Whatever you found along the way was fair game. Autumn was the time when you could walk along the roadside, pick up the branch that had come down in a windstorm, and cut a sprig of goldenrod and a stem of asters, and no one would follow you home brandishing a fist. It was all on the verge of vanishing.

But if my mother had anything to do with it, autumn would remain alive for as long as she could sustain it on our mantel or on the windowsill, in the form of souvenirs carried home from walks. Maple leaves, acorns, hickory nut husks, brown seedheads, berried branches – at other times of year she might leave them by the wayside, but in autumn they had value. Nature never really went to sleep as far as we were concerned. It was just drawn inside, closer to the family's heart.

CHAPTER FIVE

WINTER

MIRACLES ARE HARD TO FIND IN WINTER, BUT THE season presents plenty of opportunity for the endeavor. There is enough spare time to bundle up, take excursions, and make discoveries. Or you can hunker down close to home. Winter is for intimacy, for snuggling up together and reading something warm and cozy, for clasping warm mugs after snowball fights, for sinking into pillows and smelling the rush of perfume from the rosemary, sweet bay, or whatever you happen to brush with your elbow. The only plants you know in winter are houseplants, and they become close companions. But then, winter is a time of closeness.

For some reason, winter is rich with recollections. You have to find flowers; they don't just wait around every corner. So every hard-won discovery clings tenaciously to your memory. And yet winter has an opaque quality, so that all your memories of the holidays, sledding, pine cones, and greenhouse ventures are muted, as if seen through frosted glass. And they are all flavored with hot chocolate. Winter has a tough exterior, but it keeps a warm heart.

THE GREENHOUSE

LIKE MAGIC, GREENHOUSES ALWAYS UNFOLDED IN A PUFF OF vapor in winter. When you pushed open the heavy wooden door, simultaneously stamping the snow from your boots, the cold air rushed in and skirmished with the humidity inside, and for a tumultuous moment everything was wrapped in a cloud. Nothing was visible for that instant, but you could smell the distinct aroma of warm earth mingled with the moss that carpeted the dirt floor beneath the benches. Later, when the fog dispersed and you took a few steps inside, the earthy smell gave way to the combined perfumes of citrus, jasmine, old florist roses, and Parma violets. When you get to know it, every greenhouse has its own essence.

My mother didn't take me to Mrs. Logee's greenhouse. I discovered the crystal kingdom myself en route to sledding or ice skating. The big glass building seemed warm and invitingly empty, and my curiosity had to be satisfied. So I pushed open that heavy wooden door and made the first of many vapor-wrapped entrances into the jungle.

That's exactly how Mrs. Logee's greenhouse lingers in my mind's eye: a tangle of tall stems and dangling trumpet flowers, a cacophony of brazen colors sequestered under glass in the midst of bitter winter. A maze of aisles encroached on by groping vines, a labyrinth of little nooks and crannies that dead-ended abruptly in a wall of creeping fig or myrtle sprigs—that was the greenhouse. Its voice was the drip of hoses left running to soak the soil beneath the camellias, the hum of fans whirring in the background, and the occasional crash of last night's snow sliding down the warm panes.

Everyone entered the greenhouse in a rush of cold air, so it invariably took a few nervous seconds to reassure myself that it was in fact Mrs. Logee who had pushed open the wooden door behind me. When I could make out her voluminous, threadbare wool coat, she'd be wiping the steam from her glasses, seemingly oblivious to the fact that I was inside, despite the telltale sled waiting outside the door.

After she'd shaken the snow from her coat and replaced the broom she used to beat the heavy snow from the boughs along the road, Mrs. Logee put me to work. She always found something for me to do: collect camellia blossoms from the paths or, worse, rake the paths, serenaded by the steady thump, thump, thump as she potted plants at the

bench in the far corner. Later, when I'd gained her trust, I was permitted to pick violets and then sit on the far side of the office counter as her old but still fleet fingers fashioned them into wreaths.

In the corner of the office sat Mr. Logee, the visor of his dusty green cap stuck with an arsenal of florist pins and pulled down low on his brow while he snoozed silently in the creaky old chair by the desk. At first I thought that he probably shared the disposition of my torpid cat, napping the afternoon away, until someone mentioned that he stoked the greenhouse furnaces all night.

I spent many winter afternoons in that greenhouse, wandering beneath banana trees and palm fronds and watching Mrs. Logee's nimble hands as they repotted plants, wrapped evergreens around moss frames, or wired boutonnières. Countless hours disappeared as I listened to the story of how the greenhouse blew into the neighbor's yard in a hurricane but Mr. Logee caught every pane of glass unbroken, not even cracked or chipped, as it went flying through the air.

I heard about the monkey puzzle tree, about angel's trumpets and mosquito flowers. I learned about the snail flower, which only bumblebees could pollinate, and the night-blooming cereus, which lured bats with its eerie aroma. While listening, I watched hands that were comfortable with plants, that never hesitated to prune and divide and smash broken pots into crockery shards or to shake a finger in my direction when I inadvertently created more broken pots.

I scooped up fistfuls of begonia soil and felt precisely how it differed from geranium mix. And I became part of the rhythms, and was thankful that the untidy camellias which littered their petals all over my freshly raked aisles only blossomed for a few brief months in midwinter. But that was when I knew the greenhouse most intimately—when it was frozen outdoors but wonderfully toasty and sun-drenched inside.

Mrs. Logee never had a bottomless reserve of patience for little girls and their constant questions, so at some point she would put down a corsage half finished, descend the office steps into the bowels of the greenhouse, and emerge with a violet or a rosemary sunk in a stout clay pot. Then she'd entrust it to me with stern warnings about how quickly I'd have to run directly home, not stopping to dawdle, so the little denizen from the tropics wouldn't be chilled.

CAMELLIAS

IN WINTER, YOU COULD SEE YOUR BREATH IN THE GREENHOUSE where the camellias grew. Early in the morning, before the sun came streaming through the glass, or on bitter afternoons when snow still stuck to the panes, I had to rake the aisles wearing mittens and a sweater. I always wondered how those camellias survived where I shivered. But those shiny-leaved shrubs luxuriated, budding and opening such a largesse of fluffy flowers that I spent most of the winter cleaning up after them.

I had mixed emotions about camellias. On the one hand, they were bothersome, because the flowers scarcely opened fully before shattering into a pile of telltale petals when you surreptitiously tried to slip a few into your pocket. But on the other hand, they were provocative. Camellias lured you to come and visit, to reach out and run your fingers over their petals, to pluck a snow-white 'Purity' and watch its petals flutter to the ground. They were coquettish flowers, inciting detours from wherever you were bound so you could see which ones were open, what subtle variations and combinations of pink, white, blush, rose, and scarlet they had, how many were slowly unfolding and how many littered the walkways.

They were perverse flowers, to be sure, scattering their confetti at my feet. And I was thankful that they blossomed and shattered for only a few brief months when days were short, bleak, and blossom-bereft outdoors. But perhaps because it was winter, they were especially engaging, causing me to tarry, to hear stories of taffeta gowns and silk bows, of waltzes and dance cards and operas and all sorts of glittering things I could not for the life of me associate with Mrs. Logee with her threadbare wool coat and wrinkled old fingers. As I leaned against the wooden counter in the office watching her prepare camellias for New Year's Eve, the bell over the door would tinkle and in would walk someone in a cloud of cold air, and Mrs. Logee would take out her ledger, write up the order for another camellia corsage, and impale it on the nail for next Wednesday.

There was something haunting about camellias. Just as summer nights were dappled with dreams of hollyhocks and nightmares of Japanese beetles, camellias had a way of slipping into your sleeping

MAKING A CAMELLIA CORSAGE

Making a camellia corsage is simple. First, free the stem of leaves, with the exception of one lone leaf beside the blossom. Then take a thin florist wire, bend it into a crook, spear the brown calyx (the papery part that holds the petals together), feed the wire through, and curve it back down the stem. Add baby's breath or a stem of ivy, or just let the camellia stand alone. Finally, take florist tape and disguise the stem and wire by winding the tape from the flower's chin down to the bottom of the stem. Keep the corsage in the refrigerator until it's needed and then attach it to its wearer with one of those long, sharp florist pins.

hours in winter. Even more than all the summer flowers, they were unforgettable for their sheer beauty, for their glow and poise and the stories surrounding them. I would have liked to adopt one.

Like the ducklings that outgrew the bathtub a few weeks after I brought them home, camellias couldn't really be accommodated in our house. I would have gladly grown them in my bedroom, and offered as much, but my mother absolutely forbade it. So interaction with camellias was confined to visits with Mrs. Logee and time spent in the tall old greenhouse, where one aisle was monopolized by a mass of camellias joining shoulders. In winter they formed a solid hedge of flowers and stole the show. In summer they were easily overlooked.

If I found a hose running and the greenhouse bed flooded in summer, it was always to prod the camellias' winter performance and strengthen the cutting slips that Mrs. Logee would take as soon as the last blossom fell in February. If I came upon her mixing fertilizer on summer afternoons, it was invariably to feed her camellias. It was her solemn responsibility to make certain that there was always a bounty of early camellias for the holidays. If all went well, each winter morning found Mrs. Logee up early, hat and coat and galoshes caked with snow, glasses steamy, harvesting her crop of camellias for corsages.

Harvest was Mrs. Logee's domain. The petals were like satin, but they bruised at my touch. Mrs. Logee, however, stood behind the office counter hour after hour, patiently wiring the petals to the stem so they wouldn't shatter while someone was waltzing, telling stories of a time when proper young ladies wore only pure white camellias, without a blush of color. She spoke of a lost epoch when camellias were pinned at your tiny waist to accentuate the curves before the skirt flared full and wide to sweep the floor. It was later, much later, with the arrival of the flapper era and sleek fashions, that corsages moved above the heart.

I was young when I knew Mrs. Logee, too young to care much about rustling skirts, cinched waists, and the impact of a few fluffy flowers placed where they would rise and fall when your breath quickened while you whirled around the dance floor. But somehow even then I felt an affinity for camellias.

SCENTED GERANIUM CAKE

THE ONLY ADVANTAGE TO STAYING HOME SICK WAS THE prospect of spending the entire day doing nothing but watching my mother. Always warmed from the sun pouring through its wide, uncurtained windows, the kitchen was where I camped out, sniffling every once in a while just to remind everyone that I wasn't feeling well. Not that there was ever any doubt.

Even on sick days, diversions were at hand. Certain books that never surfaced when good health prevailed suddenly appeared when illness struck. Meanwhile, a stash of puzzles, games, paper dolls, and coloring books materialized from some obscure closet, held in the certainty that every childhood is punctuated by a series of ailments. I obliged by catching chicken pox, measles, mumps, and all the other maladies of youth right on schedule, as well as every cold and flu that I could gather from my classmates. All those germs and viruses provided ample opportunity to lie in the rocker by the stove on a throne of pillows and blankets, cartons of Kleenex close at hand, face flushed with fever, watching the comings and goings in the kitchen.

If you couldn't be outdoors, the kitchen was the next best place. Not only was it blessed with plenty of sunbeams, it was the place for cats to congregate. Because they sensed my debilitated state and realized that I lacked the energy even to try to stuff their fur into rollers, they threw caution to the wind and curled up in my lap to receive a good, long petting, until static electricity snapped in the air and tingled on my fingertips. And they weren't the only reliable company. Geraniums also shared the sun, brandishing their cheerful flower trusses no matter what the season. Before I began to walk, before I spoke my first syllable or realized that a world lay outside my bassinet and its immediate environs, I probably perceived the geraniums stationed on the kitchen windowsill. By the time I was out of the high chair and installed in the rocker, the geraniums and I were old friends.

Whether my mother always spent the day in the kitchen, I never knew. Certainly on sick days she was always wiping counters clean, cracking eggs, stirring things in saucepans, and bustling around the stove so that even if you could barely smell, you still managed to build up an appetite. And that was the whole idea.

My mother had ways to make us eat. Long before, she had discovered that the secret to food lay in the presentation. We didn't get
sandwiches for lunch; instead, we received masterpieces of food care-
fully arranged into pictures of trains, airplanes, tractors, flowers, or
whatever kindled her imagination. Everything in those days had a

MAKING A SCENTED GERANIUM CAKE

Use your favorite cake recipe; vanilla tastes the best. When you've buttered, floured, and readied the pan to turn in the batter, place several rose-scented geranium leaves – ones that haven't been sprayed with pesticides – along the sides and bottom of the pan. Put a little butter on the back of each leaf to stick it in place, and pull off each stem so the leaf lies flat in the pan. Smaller leaves work best – if they're under an inch in diameter, they stand a better chance of coming out intact when the cake is baked, cooled, turned upside down, and knocked out of the pan. The cake will taste like roses, and the kitchen will be infused with rose perfume. For decoration, you can use scented-leaf geranium flowers on top, but remove them before eating. The flowers are not edible.

gimmick, and cake was no exception. My mother's cakes were shaped into swans, elephants, giraffes, butterflies, and every other creature you could think of.

When you're feeling truly sick, not even cake seems enticing. On the road to recovery, a sweet tooth was generally the first signpost that appetite was restored, and proof that it was alive, well, and functional was tested with scented geranium cake. You had to be up, dressed, and capable of being trusted to help without sneezing into the batter before scented geranium cake was in the making.

If the red geraniums caught my eye early on, then scented geraniums were the first plants to capture my sense of smell. And the rose-scented geranium was the first in a long string of pelargonium relatives to come and go by windows throughout the house, releasing essential oils reminiscent of lemon, strawberry, apple, nutmeg, coconut, peppermint, ginger, and so on. Since the rose-scented geranium was essential to the geranium cake recipe, it secured a permanent place in the kitchen, beside the red zonal geraniums on the windowsill.

There wasn't really anything unique about the rose-scented geranium cake. The recipe was much like that for any other moist, sweet, spongy cake. Of course, we spent several hours gathering all the measuring spoons, mixing bowls, and beaters we needed for the endeavor, and the preparation entailed a colossal mess of splattered ingredients. When all the ingredients finally flowed together into one big bowl and the pan was readied to receive the fruits of several hours of hard, attention-diverting labor, the scented geranium was fetched from the windowsill, and its best leaves were sacrificed to the worthy cause.

In the rose-scented geranium cake process, the leaves go in first, after you've greased the tin. From that strategic spot, they proceed to send their fragrance floating up, infusing the whole cake with the smell of roses. The leaves served the same purpose as the picture of a cow on the bottom of our soup bowls, which had to be clearly visible before we were permitted to leave the table. In this case, though, the lure wasn't really necessary. When the cake came out of the oven and was turned out of its pan, the leaves on the bottom were revealed, now uppermost. At a time when the last few days had been punctuated by the tick of the kitchen clock, the reappearance of the familiar scented geranium leaves was no small thrill.

AMARYLLIS

MARYLLISES TURNED UP IN THE MOST UNLIKELY PLACES. They had a grandeur that seemed most comfortable among Aubusson rugs, polished wood floors, and front parlors, but I encountered my first amaryllis at the Burtons' farmhouse when someone had to fetch a last-minute quart of fresh Jersey milk. The Burtons never fussed much over the Fourth of July, but by the time December rolled around and their farm was buried under a few feet of snow, they were ready to celebrate a holiday.

I remember that evening clearly. Matthew pulled his barn coat on and shuffled out to the refrigerator where the extra bottles of milk were kept (the ones that Joan didn't need for making tomorrow morning's pancakes), shooing away the many cats that wound around his legs as he walked. He wasn't out the door long before Joan beckoned me into the part of the house that she'd decorated.

Imagine the surroundings. The farmhouse was proud, but not fancy. Even the smartest room was fairly utilitarian, since the Burtons had neither time nor inclination for frivolity – except a little during December. There was a tree, with no blinking lights, tinsel, or strings of popcorn, just a few handmade hollowed-out eggs with windows cut so you could see the painted insides. All of Matthew's farm journals, dog-eared and yellow from affectionate handling, were tucked in a corner; and every *Farmer's Almanac* ever published was where it could be readily consulted, just in case there was a difference of opinion about the weather. But these elements faded into the shadows, since the room was lit only by two lamps, one over the chair where Matthew read and one like a spotlight over the table holding the amaryllis.

By that time I was fairly worldly. I'd been to a botanical garden and attended every white elephant sale that the PTA put on. But I'd never seen anything like the amaryllis before. It looked like something from outer space crossed with an air-raid siren; its huge blossoms were certainly fully capable of intercepting messages from planets near and far.

Like all firsts, this amaryllis never faded from my memory. The color was blood red, a deep, rich shade spread over a silken surface. All four blossoms on the rigid spike were open simultaneously, and if it had any leaves at all, they certainly weren't drawing attention from those larger-than-life flowers.

ENCOURAGING AMARYLLISES

Amaryllises pose no challenge if you receive bulbs ready for planting shortly before the holidays. Just plant the bulb in any potting soil, leaving the top third exposed; water the pot when the soil is dry to the touch and provide warm temperatures (above 60 degrees Fahrenheit). A blossom spike is bound to begin jutting out in a few brief weeks. Encouraging flowers in successive years is not quite so simple. After the plant flowers, keep the foliage growing with good light, regular watering (but not soggy conditions), and fertilizer every few weeks throughout the summer. Toward the end of the season, dry off the bulb by withholding water to force it into dormancy. Store it in a dark, cool (not cold) place until the winter holidays are pending, and then begin the cycle again.

Always willing to talk at length on any topic, Joan gave me a short history of the plant's habits, difficulties, and date of birth. Joan didn't call it an amaryllis, of course. To her it was simply a Christmas lily, probably not a Barbados lily and definitely not the hippeastrum of horticulturists. Without urging or inquiry, she explained why it wasn't prominent in summer. She undoubtedly rattled on about not watering during dormancy or which cousin on her husband's side had given them the plant in the first place, but I wasn't listening. If anything is capable of dumbfounding, it's an amaryllis.

Joan mentioned a second spike later in winter, and that did sink in. I made a mental note that I would have to concoct some good excuse to stop by when the second coming was predicted, because it seemed implausible that such a surreal event could possibly be reproduced. I had learned to be skeptical, even of nature.

Plenty of amaryllises followed over the years. I found them in rich, lavish homes, beside grand pianos, flanking grand staircases, and beneath magnificent chandeliers. But none equaled the impact of the amaryllis in the farmhouse. I didn't tell anyone about it when I got home, because they wouldn't believe me. Some things are best kept to yourself.

TAKING ROOT

YOU PROBABLY HAVE MANY MEMORIES OF YOUR FORMATIVE years. You can probably recall flying kites and jumping waves. But isn't it the perfume of that rose floating through an open window at dusk that clings most firmly to your memory? Don't you remember all the afternoons when you got your knees muddy while fumbling through the flowerbeds your mother was trying to plant? I do.

My mother would never qualify among the ranks of ardent gardeners. But she loved a nice flowerbed, and she passed that along to me. It took root, and together we blossomed.

ACKNOWLEDGMENTS

So many people have shared in the creation of this book, and we thank them all. We would like to thank our agent, Colleen Mohyde; our editor, Frances Tenenbaum; our manuscript editor, Liz Duvall; and the book's designer, Susan McClellan.

We would like to thank all the people who opened their homes, gardens, vintage pickups, and hearts to us, most especially Kit and Marty Sagendorf, Logee's Greenhouses, Peter Wooster, Kathy Barlow, Wendy Walker and Chris Brigham, Tasha Tudor, the Bellamy-Ferriday House and Garden, Yaddo, "The Vale" at the Lyman Estate, Maple Bank Farm, Frank and Anne Cabot, Rachel Kane, Debbie Deal, Barbara and Charles Robinson, Missy Stevens and Tommy Simpson, the late J. Watson Webb, and Rick Peters. We are grateful to those who lent us clothing, most especially Casco Bay Wool Works, April Cornell, and numerous antique clothes collectors, as well as Lucinda Rooney, who provided the May baskets.

Most especially we are grateful to the mothers and daughters who modeled for and inspired this book: Cyd Sellars and Brenna and Kiernan Sellars, Stephanie Kahane and Lea Kahane, Wendy Walker and Riley and Eve Brigham, Gaila Rossiter and Bonnie Rae Rossiter, Toni Hays and Courtney Hays, Kathy Barlow and Kate and Emma Barlow, Susan McClellan and Willa Koerner, Sharon Hodder and Nikyla and Jessica Hodder, Carole Mackay and Kelsey Mackay, Ann Novak and Sarah Novak, Joy Logee Martin, Susannah Brown, Josie Gombas, Janice Herrick, Rochell Leah Gregoire, and Claire Wescott.

Tovah adds a special note of thanks to Joy Logee Martin, her mentor, who taught her everything she knows about gardening. And she dedicates this book to her mother, Selma W. Eigner, who shaped her world long before she thought to pick up a pen and who encouraged an overactive imagination both past and present. Richard Brown dedicates this book to the memory of his mother, Marjory Brown.